MW01234430

GREAT SPORTS TEAMS

THE ATLANTA BRAVES

JOHN F. GRABOWSKI

LUCENT
BOOKS ®

GALE

San Diego • Detroit • New York • San Francisco • Cleveland
New Haven, Conn. • Waterville, Maine • London • Munich

For more information, contact
Lucent Books
27500 Drake Rd.
Farmington Hills, MI 48331-3535
Or you can visit our Internet site at http://www.gale.com

LIBRARY OF CONGRESS CATALOGING-IN-PUBLICATION DATA

Grabowski, John F.
    The Atlanta Braves / by John F. Grabowski.
        p. cm. — (Great sports teams)
Includes bibliographical references and index.
Summary: Discusses the history, formation, development, and popularity
of the Atlanta Braves baseball team, including a look at individual
players who have had an impact on the success of the team.
Includes bibliographical references and index.
    ISBN 1-59018-304-5
    1. Atlanta Braves (Baseball team)—History—Juvenile literature. 2. Baseball
players—United States—Biography—Juvenile literature. [1.Atlanta Braves (Baseball
team)—History. 2. Baseball—History.] I. Title. II. Great sports teams (Lucent Books)
    GV875.A8G73 2004
    796.357'64'09758231—dc21
                                                        2003004065

Printed in the United States of America

Contents

FOREWORD

Former Supreme Court Chief Justice Warren Burger once said he always read the sports section of the newspaper first because it was about humanity's successes, while the front page listed only humanity's failures. Millions of people across the country today would probably agree with Burger's preference for tales of human endurance, record-breaking performances, and feats of athletic prowess. Although these accomplishments are far beyond what most Americans can ever hope to achieve, average people, the fans, do want to affect what happens on the field of play. Thus, their role becomes one of encouragement. They cheer for their favorite players and team and boo the opposition.

ABC Sports president Roone Arledge once attempted to explain the relationship between fan and team. Sport, said Arledge, is "a set of created circumstances—artificial circumstances—set up to frustrate a man in pursuit of a goal. He has to have certain skills to overcome those obstacles—or even to challenge them. And people who don't have those skills cheer him and admire him." Over a period of time, the admirers may develop a rabid—even irrational—allegiance to a particular team. Indeed, the word "fan" itself is derived from the word "fanatic," someone possessed by an excessive and irrational zeal. Sometimes this devotion to a team is because of a favorite player; often it's because of where a person lives, and, occasionally, it's because of a family allegiance to a particular club.

4

Whatever the reason, the bond formed between team and fan often defies reason. It may be easy to understand the appeal of the New York Yankees, a team that has gone to the World Series an incredible thirty-eight times and won twenty-six championships, nearly three times as many as any other major league baseball team. It is more difficult, though, to comprehend the fanaticism of Chicago Cubs fans, who faithfully follow the progress of a team that hasn't won a World Series since 1908. Regardless, the Cubs have surpassed the 2 million mark in home attendance in fourteen of the last seventeen years. In fact, their two highest totals were posted in 1999 and 2000, when the team finished in last place.

Each volume in Lucent's Great Sports Teams in History series examines a team that has left its mark on the "American sports consciousness." Each book looks at the history and tradition of the club in an attempt to understand its appeal and the loyalty—even passion—of its fans. Each volume also examines the lives and careers of people who played significant roles in the team's history. Players, managers, coaches, and front-office executives are represented.

Endnoted quotations help bring the text in each book to life. In addition, all books include an annotated bibliography and a For Further Reading list to supply students with sources for conducting additional individual research.

No one volume can hope to explain fully the mystique of the New York Yankees, Boston Celtics, Dallas Cowboys, or Montreal Canadiens. The Lucent Great Sports Teams in History series, however, gives interested readers a solid start on the road to understanding the mysterious bond that exists between modern professional sports teams and their devoted followers.

INTRODUCTION

A Winning Tradition

Over the years, the Atlanta Braves franchise has undergone several changes. The team originally started out in Boston, and then moved to Milwaukee before finally settling in Atlanta. At various times, the club was known as the Doves, the Rustlers, and the Bees. The franchise has experienced many highs and lows in its long history. Since 1991, however, the ability to put an exciting, competitive team on the field has been a constant.

The Team of the Nineties

When the Milwaukee Braves relocated to Atlanta in 1966, they became the first major sports team to represent the city. The Braves won the National League West three years later to give the town its first pro sports title. Since then, they have been joined in Atlanta by the Hawks of the National Basketball Association (in 1968), the Falcons of the National Football League (1966), and the Thrashers of the National Hockey League (1999). None of these clubs has won a championship, and only the Falcons have won as much as a divisional title. (When the Braves were struggling in the 1970s, a popular bumper sticker of the day read, "Go Braves! and Take the Falcons with You!")

Since their arrival in Atlanta, the Braves have become one of the most successful teams in all of professional sports. Since 1966, they have won thirteen divisional titles, including an incredible eleven in a row from 1991 to 2002. (A players' strike cut short the 1994 season, so no champion was named.) They have won five pennants in that time, and a world championship in 1995.

America's Team

The team's success, quite naturally, has brought a jump in attendance and an increase in fan participation. Beginning in 1991, Braves games have been punctuated at key points by the

Atlanta's David Justice scores the winning run in Game 3 of the 1991 World Series. Since that year, the Braves have dominated the National League.

infamous "tomahawk chop." In this somewhat politically in-
correct move, thousands of fans begin moving their hands—
which may or may not be holding a red foam tomahawk—in a
chopping motion while doing an eerie chant along with the or-
gan music. Whether the "chop" disrupts the play of opposing
players is open to conjecture, but the feeling of camaraderie it
engenders among the participants cannot be denied.

The love affair between the Braves and their fans is not limited to the Atlanta area. The team's games have been telecast
over the Turner Broadcasting System cable network since the
mid-1970s, allowing baseball fans all across the country to follow the exploits of Chipper Jones, Greg Maddux, Gary
Sheffield, and company. This wide exposure, together with the
club's success, has enabled the Braves to become baseball's ver-
sion of America's Team.

CHAPTER 1

Three Cities, Three Championships

Professional baseball in the United States dates back to 1869 with the formation of the Cincinnati Red Stockings, the first team composed entirely of professional players. Two years later, the first professional league came into existence. One of the ten charter members of the National Association of Professional Base Ball Players was the Boston Red Stockings. That team eventually evolved into the present-day Atlanta Braves, a club that has won championships while representing three different cities. As such, the Braves are the oldest continuously operating team in professional sports history.

An Early Powerhouse

The Cincinnati Red Stockings were founded by Harry Wright—known as the Father of Professional Baseball—in 1869. The team dominated baseball in the early days, winning the first eighty-nine games they played. One of their games in Boston was witnessed by a businessman named Ivers Whitney Adams. Adams became intrigued with the idea of building a Boston team of the same caliber as the mighty Cincinnati club. He got his chance when the Red Stockings reverted to amateur status

9

A nineteenth-century illustration of the Boston Red Stockings baseball club.
The Red Stockings eventually changed their name to the Braves and moved
from Boston to Milwaukee before heading south to Atlanta.

following the 1870 season due to financial difficulties. The
players were now open to offers from other teams.

On January 20, 1871, Adams formed the Boston Red Stockings Club. Adams served as president, and he hired Wright to
find players for the new team. Wright did so by signing several
of his former Cincinnati teammates. On March 17, payment of a
$10 membership fee earned the team a position in the National
Association, a newly formed professional baseball league.

Adams leased a playing field called the Union Base Ball
Ground for the team's home games. The club began play in
1871 and won twenty of thirty games to finish in second place
behind the Philadelphia Athletics. Over the next four seasons,
the Red Stockings finished in first place each year, dominating
the competition. Boston won 205 of 255 games over that span
of time, led by pitching ace Al Spalding.

By 1875, the National Association was in trouble. The Red
Stockings' domination of the league caused seven of the thir-

teen teams that began play that season to fold due to lack of attendance. The league itself ceased operations after the 1875 season.

Early the next year, a new circuit was organized by former Chicago White Stockings president William A. Hulbert. The National League of Professional Base Ball Clubs came into existence on February 2, 1876. The Boston Red Stockings of Nathaniel T. Apollonio (who had directed the team's operations during its final two seasons of play in the National Association) became one of the new league's charter members.

The Beaneaters

The Red Stockings played in the first game in National League history, defeating the Philadelphia Athletics, 6-5, on April 22, 1876. The team finished in fourth place that year. Prior to the start of the 1877 season, Arthur H. Soden was installed as the club's new president. Soden would remain in control of the team for the next three decades. During that time, it would win a total of eight pennants, more than any other club over that period.

Five of those pennants were won from 1891 to 1898. By that time, Soden's charges were known as the Beaneaters, a nickname coined by sportswriters who believed Red Stockings to be too similar to the Red Legs of Cincinnati. The team was so dominant in 1893, New York Giants manager John Montgomery Ward maintained, "The Bostons could have beaten any all-star nine the league could have put together this season."[1] Among that team's top players were outfielders Hugh Duffy and Tommy McCarthy, and pitcher Kid Nichols.

The Beaneaters' golden era ended with the turn of the century. Over the next decade, the team changed ownership and struggled along first as the Doves (under brothers George S. and John S. Dovey) and then as the Rustlers (under president William Hepburn Russell). When James E. Gaffney took over in 1912, he renamed the club the Braves (Gaffney had political connections with New York's Tammany Hall politicians, who were often referred to as "braves" for the Delaware Indian chief after which the Tammany Society was named).

The Miracle Braves

Following the team's fourth consecutive last-place finish in 1912, the Braves advanced to fifth place the next year under manager George Stallings. By midseason of 1914, the club was back in last place. "This bunch of mine is the worst looking ball club I've ever seen,"[2] said Stallings.

From July 18 on, however, the team could do no wrong. The Braves went 51–16 over the second half of the season. Short-stop Walter "Rabbit" Maranville sparked the club to a first-place finish, earning the squad the nickname the Miracle Braves. The team moved on to the World Series, where their opponents were Connie Mack's mighty Philadelphia Athletics, who had compiled the best record in baseball.

The heavily favored Athletics took the National League champions lightly. Said pitcher Chief Bender, who had been assigned by Mack to scout the Braves, "We don't need to scout that bush-league outfit."[3] Bender could not have been more wrong. The Braves received timely hitting and excellent pitching, and limited the powerful Athletics to a .172 batting average. The Braves swept all four games from Philadelphia (the first such four-game sweep in Series history) to cap their season with an upset of monumental proportions. The victory gave them their first World Series championship and a permanent place in baseball lore.

Bleak Times

The Braves remained competitive over the next two seasons, finishing second in 1915 and third in 1916. The former year also saw them unveil their new 43,500-seat home field, Braves Park. The United States' entry into World War I in 1917, however, marked the beginning of the bleakest period in franchise history. In the twenty-nine years from 1917 to 1945, the Braves finished with a winning record just five times. Only three times did the club end the year in the first division.

Over that span, the Braves were directed from the front office by five different presidents, and on the field by ten different managers. Unfortunately, none of these men could bring the Braves back into contention. In 1936, new club president

Boston shortstop Walter "Rabbit" Maranville led the Braves to their first World Series victory. Maranville spent much of his Hall of Fame career in Boston.

Bob Quinn decided a change in nickname was what the team needed. The Braves became the Bees, and Braves Field was renamed National League Park (or more informally, the Beehive). When it became obvious that the nickname was not the problem, the team reverted back to the name Braves in 1941.

Spahn and Sain and Pray for Rain

In 1946, Boston Braves owner Lou Perini (who had been part of a group that bought the Braves two years earlier) hired Billy Southworth as manager. Southworth had won three pennants while with the St. Louis Cardinals, and Perini thought he was the man who could rejuvenate the Braves and bring them back to respectability.

With Perini's blessing, Southworth began acquiring players who would form the core of the next Boston pennant winner. Shortstop Alvin Dark, first baseman Johnny Hopp, and pitcher Warren Spahn joined the club in 1946, the same season in which pitcher Johnny Sain returned from the service. The Braves finished in fourth place that season with a record of 81–72.

The next year, slugging third baseman Bob Elliott came over from the Pittsburgh Pirates. He batted .317 with 22 home runs and 113 runs batted in to win the Most Valuable Player award in his first year with Boston. Spahn and Sain developed into the league's best pitching duo, and the Braves moved up to third place with their best record in thirty-one years.

Long-suffering Braves fans were finally rewarded for their patience in 1948. Shortstop Dark, second baseman Eddie Stanky, and outfielders Jeff Heath, Tommy Holmes, and Mike McCormick all batted over .300, but the strength of the team was its pitching. Led by Spahn and Sain (the phrase "Spahn

Warren Spahn (left) and Johnny Sain were aces for the Braves during the 1948 season. The pair combined for thirty-nine wins that year.

and Sain and pray for rain" was born during this period, referring to the fact that the pair were the only starting pitchers on whom the team could depend), the staff posted the best earned run average in the league.

The Braves finished the season in first place, six and a half games ahead of Southworth's former club, the Cardinals. Boston's opponent in the World Series that fall was the Cleveland Indians, who had defeated the Boston Red Sox in a one-game playoff for the American League pennant. The Braves could not duplicate the success of their 1914 brethren and lost the Series in six hard-fought games. After having gone more than three decades without appearing in postseason play, however, the season was still considered to be a rousing success.

The Road to Milwaukee

Unfortunately, the Braves' success was short-lived. Southworth's hard-driving ways caused dissension among some of the players, and the team dropped to fourth place in 1949 with a record of 75–79. The club failed to improve over the next couple of years, and attendance fell drastically. Boston fans turned their attention to the American League Red Sox, who annually produced a team that was a stronger contender than the Braves.

The Braves fell to seventh place in 1952. Attendance for the year was a pathetic 281,278, with the final game drawing a pitiful crowd of only 8,822. As the monetary losses mounted, Perini and his brothers Joseph and Charles were busy buying up the stock of minority stockholders in the team. Speculation arose that the club would be moved to Milwaukee, home of the Braves' top farm team.

On March 13, 1953, with spring training already under way, Perini announced the move. National League owners gave their formal approval five days later, and the Boston Braves were history.

An Instant Hit

The announcement of the move sent the city of Milwaukee into a state of wild celebration as they prepared to greet their new heroes. The team that began the 1953 season bore little resemblance to the club that finished in seventh place the year before. Catcher Del Crandall and pitchers Johnny Antonelli and Bob Buhl returned from the service, outfielder Andy Pafko and first baseman Joe Adcock were acquired in trades, and outfielder Billy Bruton was promoted from the minors.

The Braves began the season with a 2-0 win in Cincinnati. They returned to Milwaukee and opened new County Stadium before a standing-room crowd of 34,357. The fans went away happy as the Braves pulled out a ten-inning, 3-2 win over the Cardinals on Bruton's first major-league home run (and only one of the year).

Led by Spahn's pitching and the slugging of second-year third baseman Eddie Mathews (who led the league in home runs), the Braves finished in second place behind the Brooklyn Dodgers. The club's exciting play helped it set a National League attendance record by drawing 1,826,297 fans that season.

World Champions

The Braves continued to field contending teams over the next several years. Rookie outfielder Hank Aaron joined the team in 1954 and helped the club to eighty-nine wins and a third-place finish. The Braves also became the first National League team to attract 2 million spectators that year.

Milwaukee finished second to the Dodgers in both 1955 and 1956, falling just one game shy of the top spot in the latter year. The next year, manager Fred Haney obtained second baseman Red Schoendienst from the Giants. The veteran's presence proved to be just what the team needed. The Braves won the National League pennant by eight games and advanced to the World Series to face the New York Yankees.

Pitcher Lew Burdette was Milwaukee's hero in the Fall Classic. He tied a Series record by defeating the New Yorkers three times, including a 5-0 shutout in Game 7 to give the Braves the championship. Aaron was the club's hitting star, batting .393 with 3 home runs and 7 runs batted in.

The Braves duplicated their regular-season success in 1958. They again won the pennant by eight games, thereby earning successive National League titles for the first time since 1897–98. Their opponent in the Series, once again, was the

Braves third baseman Eddie Mathews warms up before a game. After moving from Boston in 1953, the team drew more than 1.8 million fans.

Yankees. When Milwaukee won three of the first four contests, it appeared a second straight championship was at hand. The New Yorkers, however, bounced back to win the next three games to defeat the Braves.

Milwaukee finished the 1959 season in a tie for first place with Los Angeles (Brooklyn had relocated in California after the 1957 season). Their bid for a third consecutive pennant was ended when they lost a best-of-three playoff to the Dodgers. After another second-place finish in 1960, the Braves began to drop in the standings. Although the team compiled winning records in each of its final five seasons in Milwaukee (1961–65), it never again finished higher than fourth place.

The End of a Love Affair

By 1963, the honeymoon between the Braves and the city of Milwaukee had ended. Attendance had dropped significantly and rumors of a possible franchise shift began making the rounds. In March 1964, the mayor of Atlanta, Georgia, announced that a major-league team had committed to move there if a new stadium were built. Although the Braves denied any such plans, most people believed it was only a matter of time before the team headed south.

In mid-October of that year, team officials finally admitted to having received a lease offer from Atlanta. National League owners met to discuss the planned shift, and on November 7, 1964, the move was approved—but for 1966, when the team's lease in Milwaukee was up, not 1965. Although the Braves fielded a contending team in 1965, resentment over the future move caused fans to stay away from the games. Several contests drew fewer than one thousand paying spectators. The Braves' thirteen-year run in Milwaukee ended on September 22. Just over 12,500 fans came out to see the team drop an eleven-inning 7-6 decision to the Dodgers.

The Move South

The Braves' first home game in Atlanta Stadium was attended by a near-capacity crowd of 50,671. The team fell to the Pirates, 3-2, in thirteen innings in its debut. By the end of the year, Atlanta had hit a franchise-record 207 home runs, led by Aaron (44), Joe Torre (36), and Felipe Alou (31). The Braves could manage only a fifth-place finish, however, as the pitching staff struggled. Despite its mediocre performance, the club was a success at the box office, drawing 1,539,801 fans, its highest attendance since 1959.

The Braves did not post another winning record until 1969. That year, the National League was divided into two divisions to accommodate new franchises in Montreal and San Diego.

Playing in the National League West, the Braves won their division by three games over the San Francisco Giants. Atlanta's hopes for a pennant were ended by the Miracle Mets, who swept the Braves in three games in the National League Championship Series (NLCS).

The Braves teams of the early 1970s were known for their solid hitting and weak pitching. The 1973 club was the first team in history to have three hitters—Davey Johnson, Darrell Evans, and Aaron—slug forty or more home runs. The team still finished next to last in the West, however, as the pitchers recorded a team earned run average of 4.25.

Ted Turner Arrives

The Braves muddled through the mid-1970s showing few signs of improvement. The most excitement on the field was generated by Hank Aaron's pursuit of Babe Ruth's career home run record. Aaron finally surpassed Ruth in the team's first home game of 1974.

After posting its third losing record in four years in 1975, the Braves were sold to cable television billionaire Ted Turner for an estimated $12 million. "I bought the Braves because I'm tired of seeing them kicked around," said Turner. "I'm the little guy's hero."[4]

Turner hired Dave Bristol as the team's new manager and signed free agent Andy Messersmith as its new pitching ace. Atlanta Stadium was renamed Atlanta–Fulton County Stadium and plans were made to fill it in any way possible. "I want this team to be like McDonald's," said Turner. "I want an atmosphere that will make kids want to come to the ballpark."[5]

The team staged one imaginative promotion after another in an effort to attract fans. Fan Appreciation Day, Old Timers Day, and Bat Day were joined by Wedlock and Headlock Night, the Great Baseball Nose Push, and the Cash Scramble.

All the changes, however, could not improve the team on the field. The Braves finished last in the West in 1976, then repeated their dismal performance in each of the next three seasons. Among the few bright spots for Atlanta were the play of third baseman Bob Horner, outfielders Dale Murphy and Gary Matthews, and pitcher Phil Niekro.

Baseball's all-time home run king, Hank Aaron, sits with Atlanta Braves owner Ted Turner during a 1976 game. Since Turner purchased the club in 1975, the Braves have become one of the most successful teams in baseball.

From Respectability to the Depths

Bobby Cox was hired to replace Bristol as manager in 1978. The team began to show improvement under his leadership and rose to fourth place in 1980. The improvement was not enough to satisfy Turner, however, and Cox was fired following the 1981 season.

With Joe Torre installed as manager, the Braves edged past the Dodgers to finish 1982 at the top of the National League West standings. They were quickly eliminated by the Cardinals in the NLCS, but hopes for the future were bright. Over the next two seasons, the Braves posted a pair of second-place finishes. Appreciative Atlanta fans came out in record numbers, with a franchise-high 2,119,935 passing through the gates in 1983.

Unfortunately, the Braves' success was only temporary. Young players like outfielder Brad Komminsk and first baseman Gerald

Perry failed to live up to expectations and the pitching staff continued to struggle. Torre was fired, but Eddie Haas, Bobby Wine, and Chuck Tanner had no more luck as his successors.

In an effort to right their sinking ship, Atlanta rehired Cox, but this time as general manager. He concentrated on developing the team's farm system, particularly young pitchers like Tom Glavine, Steve Avery, and Kent Mercker. After last-place finishes in 1988, 1989, and 1990 (by which time Cox had moved back into the managerial role), the Braves were ready to make their move.

Worst to First

The franchise's young players came on strong in 1991, fueling a turnaround of remarkable proportions. Outfielders Ron Gant and David Justice and third baseman Terry Pendleton led the offense, while Glavine, Avery, Charlie Leibrandt, and John Smoltz anchored the pitching staff. Under Cox's leadership, the 1991 club won a remarkable twenty-nine games more than the previous year's team and finished first in the division. Not since the modern era began in 1903 had a team rebounded from finishing with the worst record in the league one year to leading its division the next.

Atlanta proceeded to defeat Pittsburgh in the NLCS to advance to the World Series where they faced the Minnesota Twins. With the Braves leading, three games to two, the Twins won the final two games of the Series, both in extra innings. Atlanta's quest for a world championship fell short, but Braves' fans could not complain. The team's journey from worst to first was one of the great achievements in franchise history.

An Incredible Run

No one knew it at the time, but the Braves' 1991 National League West title marked the start of one of the most amazing streaks in professional sports annals. Over the next eleven years, Atlanta won their division every season, giving them an incredible eleven straight crowns. (The players' strike ended the Braves' 1994 season after 114 games. Because the rest of the season—as well as the playoffs and World Series—was canceled, there were no official division champions named.

Playing their first season in the National League East, the Braves were in second place when play was suspended, six games behind the first-place Montreal Expos.)

The backbone of the Braves' teams of this period was its outstanding pitching staff. Greg Maddux, Glavine, and Smoltz won a remarkable six Cy Young Awards (given to the best pitcher of the year in each league) among them (Maddux won another prior to joining Atlanta). Solid hitting and sound defense were also Atlanta trademarks.

The Braves surpassed the one-hundred-win mark five times during this stretch, notching a franchise-record 106 victories in 1998. They made it all the way to the World Series five times—in 1991, 1992, 1995, 1996, and 1999.

In 1995, the Braves' opponent in the Fall Classic was the Cleveland Indians. With Atlanta leading the Series, three games to two, Glavine took the mound in Game 6. He pitched one of the greatest games in World Series history, limiting the powerful Indians to one hit and no runs in eight innings. David Justice's solo home run in the sixth inning was the only run of the night. It was enough to bring the Braves their third world championship, and the city of Atlanta its first championship in any major professional sport.

The Braves were the most dominant National League team in the last decade of the twentieth century. With players like Chipper and Andruw Jones, Gary Sheffield, and Rafael Furcal leading the way, they have begun the new millennium intent on continuing that dominance.

CHAPTER 2

Hank Aaron

Hammerin' Hank Aaron is baseball's all-time home run king. He was more than just a home run hitter, however, winning a pair of batting titles and three Gold Glove awards for fielding excellence in a twenty-three-year big-league career. Baseball's all-time leader in several categories, he was named to the Baseball Hall of Fame in 1982.

The Superstar from Mobile

Henry Louis Aaron was born on February 5, 1934, in a predominantly black area of Mobile, Alabama, known as Down the Bay. He was the third of eight children born to Herbert and Estella Aaron. When Henry was eight years old, the family moved to a village known as Toulminville, just outside the Mobile city limits. There, his father worked as a boilermaker's assistant in a shipyard while his mother stayed home to take care of the kids. To make extra money, Herbert also ran a tavern located near their house.

As a youngster, Henry loved playing baseball. He would swing at bottle caps using a broom handle, something he later credited with helping him develop as a hitter. "A bottle cap will

During his major-league career, Hank Aaron pounded more home runs than any player in baseball history. Consistency was an important part of his success: Although he never hit 50 homers in a single season, he recorded 20 or more in 20 consecutive seasons.

swerve at the last instant," he explained. "You've got to go out and get it."[6] In Toulminville, he spent much of his time playing ball at Carver Park, located a block away from his home.

Henry did not play baseball in high school since Central High did not have a team. He did, however, play football and fast-pitch softball. He was a good hitter even though he batted cross-handed (with his left hand on top, which was unusual for a right-handed batter). As he explains in his autobiography, "We were never told the right way to bat. . . . I realized that I batted differently than other guys, but it felt right and it worked, so I saw no reason to change."[7]

While playing sandlot ball (informal games played outside of an organized team) in high school, Henry was spotted by Ed Scott, who managed a semipro baseball team called the Mobile Black Bears. Scott offered Henry the chance to play shortstop for the Bears and Henry accepted. The youngster was paid ten dollars for each game. Impressed by his abilities, Scott eventually recommended Aaron to the Indianapolis Clowns of the Negro American League. The skinny 150-pound teenager signed for a $200 monthly salary and left home to play for the Clowns at the age of eighteen.

From the Clowns to the Braves

Until major league baseball became integrated in 1947, the top black stars were limited to playing in the Negro leagues. By

1952, however, those leagues had begun to die out. The only way a team could make some money was by selling players to organized baseball. With Aaron showing exceptional talent for hitting a baseball, Clowns' owner Syd Pollock soon found an interested buyer in the Boston Braves (whose scout Dewey Griggs suggested to Aaron that he uncross his hands when he hit).

The Braves paid the Clowns $7,500 for the young infielder and sent him to play second base with their farm team in Eau Claire, Wisconsin. Aaron was an immediate sensation there. He batted .336 with 9 home runs and 61 runs batted in (RBIs) in

Aaron fields a ball during his 1953 season with the Jacksonville Tars, a minor-league affiliate of the Braves. That year, he was the South Atlantic League's MVP, batting .362 with 44 home runs and 125 RBIs.

eighty-seven games to earn Northern League Rookie of the Year honors.

In 1953, Aaron and teammates Felix Mantilla and Horace Garner were assigned to the Braves' Class A Jacksonville Tars farm team to break the color line in the South Atlantic League. Despite being subjected to a barrage of racial epithets, Aaron led the league in runs, hits, doubles, RBIs, and batting average and was named the circuit's Most Valuable Player.

The next year, Aaron went to spring training with the Braves. He was scheduled to begin the season in the minors, but when outfielder Bobby Thomson broke his leg, Aaron got his chance. (He had been switched to the outfield after experiencing fielding problems at second base.) He started in left field in Thomson's place the next day, and by the end of spring training, he was added to the major league roster. As Thomson later said, "You just had this feeling—even then—that this guy was something special. He was far removed from the ordinary class of ballplayer, like the rest of us."[8]

The Start of a Hall of Fame Career

Aaron started the regular season as Thomson's replacement for Milwaukee (the Braves had relocated there from Boston the previous year). As he later recalled, he did not join the team with much fanfare. "My arrival in the major leagues was pretty dull," he said. "No drama, no excitement, absolutely none. I just arrived, that's all."[9] He went 0-for-5 in his debut against the Cincinnati Reds. His first major-league hit came two days later off Vic Raschi of the St. Louis Cardinals. Eight days later, he hit his first home run, also off Raschi.

Aaron batted .280 for the year, with 13 home runs and 69 runs batted in. He appeared in 122 games before his season was ended prematurely. On September 5, he broke his ankle while sliding into third base. Ironically, Thomson came in to run for him.

Aaron bounced back in 1955 to have an outstanding sophomore season. He slugged 27 home runs (the first of twenty consecutive years in which he would hit 20 or more), drove in 106 runs, scored 105, led the league with 37 doubles, and batted .314. The following year, his numbers were just as impressive.

At age twenty-two, he led the National League in batting (.328), hits (200), and doubles (34). He added 26 homers and 92 RBIs while leading the Braves to a second-place finish, just one game behind the pennant-winning Dodgers. It set the stage for his—and the Braves—breakout year of 1957.

1957

After having come so close to winning the pennant in 1956, the Braves began the 1957 season intent on bringing Milwaukee its first title. They shut out the Reds, 1-0, on opening day behind Lew Burdette's pitching and Aaron's solo home run, and quickly moved to the top of the league standings.

Milwaukee remained in first place for most of the season, with Aaron leading the way. He began "hitting for more power" (a common phrase referring to a player's increased ability to hit home runs) than he had in the past. During one stretch, he slugged seven home runs in eight days.

When center fielder Billy Bruton was injured in July, Aaron moved over to replace him. The change in positions did not affect his performance at the plate as opposing pitchers could not figure out how to get him out. "There's no book on Aaron," said Philadelphia Phillies manager Mayo Smith. "You have to pitch him like you do [New York Yankees catcher] Yogi Berra—right down the middle with everything you've got, then close your eyes."[10]

By Labor Day, the Braves led their division by eight-and-a-half-games. With a week left in the season, they were still five games ahead of the Cardinals with just six left to play. St. Louis arrived in Milwaukee for an important three-game series, needing to win all three to keep their hopes alive of making it to the playoffs.

In the first game, on September 23, the two clubs played to a 2-2 tie, sending the contest into extra innings. In the bottom half of the eleventh, Aaron stepped in to face Cardinals reliever Billy Muffett with one out and a runner on first. On Muffett's first pitch, Aaron slugged a towering home run to left-center to give the Braves the victory and clinch the pennant for Milwaukee. After circling the bases on what he later called "the most important home run I ever hit,"[11] Aaron was mobbed at home plate and carried off on the shoulders of his delirious teammates.

Aaron finished the year with 44 home runs and 132 runs batted in, leading the National League in both categories. He also topped the circuit in runs scored while finishing third in batting with an average of .322.

In the World Series that fall, the Braves faced off against the powerful Yankees. Milwaukee prevailed in an exciting seven-game Series, with Burdette winning three of the contests. Aaron batted .393, hit 3 home runs, and drove home 7 runs for the victors. The crowning touch to his magical season came

Hank Aaron proudly shows off his 1957 National League MVP Award, while Braves pitcher Warren Spahn displays his 1957 Cy Young Award. The two Milwaukee stars helped their team defeat the Yankees in a seven-game World Series that year.

after the Series when he was named the National League's Most Valuable Player.

One of A Kind

The Braves returned to the World Series in 1958 as Aaron put together another solid year at the plate. He also won the first of three consecutive Gold Gloves for fielding excellence. His smooth, gliding style of running sometimes made it look like he was not going at full speed, but he always seemed to make the play.

Aaron's batting style was just as deceptive. He was relaxed at the plate, but when the pitch was delivered, his quick wrists and powerful hands enabled him to rocket line drives to all fields. As Cardinals' pitcher Curt Simmons put it, "He's the only ballplayer I've ever seen who goes to sleep at the plate and wakes up only to swing as the pitch comes in."[12]

Aaron swung at enough pitches to hit .333 in the Series against the Yankees that fall, but the Braves came up short, losing to the New Yorkers in seven games. He did not know it at the time, but it would be his last appearance in the Fall Classic. Over the next seven seasons, the Braves would finish second twice, then drop toward the second division.

Despite the Braves' descent in the league standings, Aaron continued to cement his status as one of the game's brightest stars. He won his second batting title in 1959 while leading the league with a career-high 223 hits. During the season, he took part in a television show called *Home Run Derby*, where two players were matched up each week to see who could hit more home runs. Aaron did well on the show and earned a total of $30,000 for his appearances. It convinced him that there was more money to be made hitting home runs. As he explained, "I noticed that they never had a show called Singles Derby."[13]

Aaron learned his lesson well. He won his second home run crown in 1963, and two more RBI titles in 1960 and 1963. Over the five-year span from 1959 to 1963, he never drove home fewer than 120 runs in a season.

On August 20, 1965, Braves third baseman Eddie Mathews slugged his twenty-eighth home run of the season. It was significant because it moved Mathews and Aaron past Babe

Ruth and Lou Gehrig as the top home-run-hitting teammates of all time with a total of 794. The pair would eventually raise their total to 863. The record was one of the few highlights of the season for the Braves in their last year in Milwaukee. The following spring, the team relocated to Atlanta. It marked an important juncture in Aaron's career.

The Move to Atlanta and Pursuit of the Babe

It didn't take long for Atlanta to influence Aaron's approach to hitting. As he relates in his autobiography:

> The first time I took batting practice in Atlanta–Fulton County Stadium, I knew that my career was headed in a new direction. Atlanta was the highest city in the major leagues, as well as the hottest, and if you could get the ball into the air, there was a good chance that it wouldn't come down in the playing field. . . . I changed my batting style immediately, no longer trying to pounce on the ball and whip it in any direction but turning and pulling it toward the seats in left field.[14]

The change in style showed immediate results. Aaron tied the National League record for most home runs by June 30 and went on to lead the league for the third time in his career (each time with 44). He also drove in 127 runs to lead in that category for the fourth time.

Over the succeeding seasons, Aaron continued to pile up home runs at a prodigious pace. On July 14, 1968, he hit the five hundredth home run of his career. Little more than a year later, he stroked number 537 to move into third place on the all-time list behind Babe Ruth and Willie Mays.

The Braves made it back to the postseason that year, finishing first in the National League West. They were defeated in three straight games by the New York Mets in the League Championship Series, however, despite Aaron's solid play. He batted .357 for Atlanta, hitting a home run in each game and driving home a total of 7 runs. At age thirty-five, it would be his last appearance in postseason play.

Hank Aaron was more than just a home-run slugger. On May 17, 1970, he became the ninth player in baseball history to record 3,000 hits; he finished his career with 3,771 hits.

On May 17, 1970, Aaron reached another milestone when he got the three thousandth hit of his career. Two months later, he hit his thirtieth home run of the season to set a league record for most seasons (twelve) with 30 or more.

The following season saw Aaron hit several significant home runs. He became the third player in history to reach 600 homers when he hit a home run against San Francisco's Gaylord Perry on April 27. Three months later, he hit the first All-Star home run of his career. When he connected for the fortieth time that season in mid-August, it established a National League mark for most seasons (seven) with 40 or more. He capped his season on September 26 with his forty-seventh blast of the year for a new personal high.

Aaron was thirty-eight years old when the 1972 season started. He continued his assault on Babe Ruth's career home run mark by clouting 34 to move past Willie Mays into second place on the all-time list. By this time, Aaron was receiving hundreds of letters a day. Much of it was hate-mail—including several death threats—from white fans who resented the fact that a black player was approaching Ruth's hallowed record. Aaron was determined to break the record as his way of quieting the bigots. "I don't care if they boo," he said, "They pay their money, and they're entitled to that. But they call me nigger and every other word you can imagine. I just won't take that."[15]

How many home runs were fueled by Aaron's anger is impossible to know. He did hit 40 more in 1973, however, and finished the season with 713, just one short of Ruth.

April 8, 1974

The 1974 season began with controversy. Atlanta opened with a three-game series against the Reds in Cincinnati. The Braves' management wanted to keep Aaron out of the series so that he

(Right) Aaron watches his 714th home run sail out of the park on April 4, 1974. (Bottom) Four days later, after breaking Babe Ruth's record with a homer off Al Downing, the jubilant slugger hugs his mother.

could set the record in front of the hometown fans. The announcement caused an uproar among some members of the media who believed such maneuvering was improper. In a highly unusual move, baseball Commissioner Bowie Kuhn ordered the Braves to use Aaron "in the same pattern of 1973, when he started approximately two of every three games."[16]

The Braves eventually agreed to comply with Kuhn's edict. In the opener on April 4, Aaron hit the record-tying 714th home run in his first at bat of the season. He sat out the second game, then went hitless in three at bats in the series finale.

The Braves returned to Atlanta to face the Dodgers in their home opener on April 8. In front of 53,775 fans, Aaron walked in the second inning against veteran Dodger left-hander Al Downing. When he came up again in the fourth inning, he swung at a Downing fastball and hit it over the left field fence into the Braves' bullpen, where it was caught by Atlanta relief pitcher Tom House. "It wasn't one of my better ones," Aaron later said of the homer. "I hit it fairly good, though, and the wind helped to carry it."[17]

Aaron circled the bases to the cheers of the crowd. He was greeted at home plate by teammates, fans, and his mother, who had been escorted out of the stands. Baseball had a new home run king.

The End of the Line

Aaron added 19 more homers to his total and finished the year with 733. Unable to guarantee him the playing time he wished for the next year, the Braves traded him after the season to the Milwaukee Brewers of the American League in exchange for outfielder Dave May. Aaron stroked 12 home runs in his return to Milwaukee in 1975, playing mainly as a designated hitter. After hitting 10 more in 1976 at the age of forty-two, Aaron announced his retirement from the game.

In addition to retiring as baseball's all-time leader in home runs with 755, Aaron also left as the leader in runs batted (2,297), total bases (6,856), and extra base hits (1,477). In addition, he ranked second in at bats (12,364) and runs scored (2,174), third in hits (3,771) and games played (3,298), and eighth in doubles (624). As he said when he made the

announcement, "I have no regrets. I've done just about everything I could. . . . I've been playing on borrowed time the last
two years. . . . It's been embarrassing for the kind of career I
had to finish my last season with a .229 average. The things I
wanted to do, I couldn't. . . . I decided the legs were gone."[18]
For his outstanding twenty-three year career, Aaron was
elected to the Baseball Hall of Fame in 1982.

The Fight for Equality

Following his retirement as an active player, Aaron returned to
the Braves with a position in the front office. He spent thirteen
years as vice president and director of player development before being appointed senior vice president and assistant to
Braves president Stan Kasten in 1989. He has remained in that
position to the current day.

Aaron spends much of his spare time working with charities
involved with sickle-cell anemia, cancer, leukemia, and cystic
fibrosis. He also gives time to the Salvation Army, Boy Scouts
of America, and Big Brothers/Big Sisters, and sponsors the
Hank Aaron Scholarship Program. Aaron has also been an out-
spoken crusader in the fight for better opportunities for African
Americans in management positions in baseball. He continues
to remain involved in the game he loves. As he explains in his
autobiography, "I wonder if I really need baseball anymore . . .
and if it really needs me. But whenever I wonder about it, I
usually come to the conclusion that I do, and it does—at least
for the time being. Baseball needs me because it needs some-
body to stir the pot, and I need it because it's my life. It's the
means I have to make a little difference in the world."[19]

CHAPTER 3

Phil Niekro

Phil Niekro is the Atlanta Braves' all-time leader in nearly every pitching category. He was the preeminent knuckleball pitcher of his time, employing the trick pitch to win 314 games in his twenty-four-year major league career. One of the most durable pitchers of all time, he hurled two hundred or more innings in a season an incredible nineteen times before retiring from the game at the age of forty-eight.

A Baseball Heritage

Philip Henry Niekro Jr. was born on April 1, 1939, in the tiny town of Blaine, Ohio. He spent most of his childhood in nearby Lansing, a larger town of about 850. Phil was the second of three children born to Philip Sr. and Ivy Niekro. (They had an older daughter, Phyllis, and a younger son, Joe, who would also become a major-league baseball player.) Like most adult males in that region of the Upper Ohio Valley—known simply as "the Valley" to those who lived there—Phil Sr. was a coal miner.

In his younger days, Phil's father had been one of the best pitchers in the area, with a blazing fastball and a strong bat.

35

"He used to pitch in the Mine Workers League," recalled Phil, "and I remember seeing and hearing accounts of him striking out 18, 19 guys in a game. He was a good first baseman, too."[20] When he was eighteen years old, however, he blew out his arm, ending his dream of someday making the major leagues. Nick McKay, another miner and former minor league catcher, taught him how to throw the knuckleball so that he was able to continue pitching. (Because the knuckleball is a pitch that is more effective when thrown with little force, it puts much less stress on the arm.) He would eventually pass on the lessons he learned to his two sons.

The Niekros were working-class people who struggled to make ends meet. They could not provide their children with a lot of material things, but made up for that by giving them an abundance of love, guidance, and affection. "I wouldn't change that time of my life in that little town for anything," said Phil. "I can't imagine anybody else enjoying growing up as much as we did."[21]

One of the things the boys shared with their father was a love of sports. "Our dad would come home at 5:00 or 5:30 from the mines," recalled Phil, "and he'd be black with coal dust. He'd go upstairs and wash and then rest for a while . . . But he'd always come down and play catch with us in the backyard. I learned to catch his knuckler before I could throw one."[22]

Phil's closest friend growing up was John Havlicek, the future basketball star of the Boston Celtics. At Bridgeport High School, the two played on the baseball, basketball, and football teams together. By that time, Phil had already learned the secret of throwing the knuckleball from his father. The pitch is actually thrown with the fingertips digging into the ball rather than the knuckles. It is released with a stiff wrist so that it comes to the plate with hardly any spin. As the air currents move over the raised seams, the ball jumps around unpredictably.

In his years at Bridgeport, Phil lost only one game as the team's pitcher. It came in the Eastern District championship game in his freshman season. The opposing pitcher for Warren Consolidated High School that day was future Pittsburgh Pirates Hall of Fame second baseman Bill Mazeroski. Despite his excellent record in high school, Phil did not attract much atten-

Although Phil Niekro could throw an assortment of pitches, he was best known for his knuckleball. The fluttering pitch helped him strike out 3,342 batters over the course of his career.

tion from major-league teams. Scouts were on the lookout for pitchers who could throw the ball ninety miles an hour, not those who relied on a trick pitch like the knuckleball.

The Long-Shot

Following his high school graduation, Phil went to work for the Continental Can Company. He continued to play legion league and semipro baseball during his spare time. About a year later, in July 1958, he received an invitation to a Milwaukee Braves tryout camp after a scout had seen him play. He attended the camp, along with about 150 other players. "The scout who ran

Niekro was a relief pitcher during his first full season with the Braves, 1965. He appeared in 41 games, posting a 2–3 record, six saves, and a 2.89 ERA.

it, Bill Baughn, signed two guys out of there," related Niekro, "me and a first baseman from West Virginia named Pete Zeck. They gave me $500, but I had to fight for that."[23]

Niekro began his pro career the next spring with Wellsville of the New York-Penn League. Over the next five years (with a year off for military service in 1963), he traveled the country, toiling for McCook of the Nebraska State League, Jacksonville of the South Atlantic League, Louisville of the American Association, Austin of the Texas League, and Denver of the Pacific Coast League. At every step along the way, the unheralded youngster had to fight to make believers out of his managers. "I was pitching with guys who signed $30,000, $40,000 bonuses," he remembered. "Why should they pay attention to someone they signed for $500? I later found out that the only guy in the organization who fought for me was Birdie Tebbetts. He kept telling the Braves, 'Stay with the kid, stay with the kid.'"[24]

At age twenty-five, Niekro finally joined the Braves for ten games in 1964 without earning a decision. In fifteen innings of relief, he compiled an earned run average of 4.80. The next year, he had a good spring training and made the team's opening day roster.

The Switch to Starter

Niekro appeared in forty-one contests for Milwaukee in 1965—all in relief—and recorded 6 saves while going 2–3. His first major-league win came on May 13 against the Pittsburgh Pirates when he hurled five innings of scoreless relief. His earned run average for the year dropped nearly two full runs, to 2.89. This was largely due to his increased mastery of the knuckleball. As his control of the pitch improved, he had to depend less and less on his other pitches, which were substantially below major-league level.

The following year, Niekro again struggled. Midway through the year, he was sent back down to Richmond for more seasoning. When he made it back to the Braves to stay in 1967, he brought a new wife, Nancy, whom he had met while at Richmond, along with him.

In June of 1967, Braves' general manager Paul Richards made Niekro into a starter. The results were impressive. He completed half of his twenty starts, winning eleven games while losing nine. In 207 innings pitched, he allowed just 164 hits and 55 walks. He credited much of his success to catcher Bob Uecker. As Niekro explained in his book *Knuckle Balls*, "He engrained in my mind that I shouldn't be afraid to throw the knuckler. What happened to it after it left my hand was not my responsibility, but instead his. As a result, he gave me that extra bit of confidence that I needed to get my career over the top."[25] An excellent defensive catcher, Uecker did his best, but still led the league with 27 passed balls because of the fluttering pitch.

Niekro's 1.87 earned run average in 1967 was a career best and good enough to lead the National League. Surprisingly, this was accomplished with a weak Atlanta team that finished in seventh place. On July 5 of that year, Phil started against his brother Joe (who had been signed by the Chicago Cubs in 1966). Phil and the Braves won the game, 8-3. It was only the second time in major league history that brothers had started against each other. (The first siblings to do so were Jesse and Virgil Barnes of the Brooklyn Dodgers and New York Giants, respectively—on May 3, 1927.)

Ace of the Staff

Niekro had another solid year in 1968, winning fourteen games with an earned run average of 2.59. It was not until the following season, however, that he really blossomed as the ace of the Atlanta staff. Niekro won a career-high twenty-three games in 1969, and was selected to the All-Star team for the first time. His final victory of the year on September 30 clinched the National League West title for the Braves. Unfortunately, his success did not carry over into the National League Championship Series. Playing the "Miracle" Mets, Niekro lost Game 1 of what would be a three-game sweep by the New Yorkers.

Niekro's performance dropped off the following year, as did that of the rest of the team. He had an emergency appendectomy during the off-season and returned to action too quickly. He never got back into peak playing shape and his record dropped to 12–18 as his earned run average ballooned to 4.27.

Niekro bounced back to win fifteen games in 1971, but the Braves struggled to stay respectable. In the twelve-year period from 1971 to 1982, Atlanta would finish with a winning record just three times; in four of those seasons, they would finish in last place. Niekro would be one of the team's few shining lights. He led the staff in wins nine times, while compiling a losing record only twice.

Despite the Braves' poor play during that stretch, Niekro provided Atlanta fans with several memorable moments. One of those occurred on August 5, 1973. That day, he became the first Atlanta Braves pitcher to toss a no-hitter as he defeated the San Diego Padres by a score of 9-0.

The following year was arguably Niekro's best. He won twenty games for the second time, tying the Dodgers' Andy Messersmith for the league lead. He also topped the circuit in complete games and innings pitched while finishing second in earned run average and shutouts. (Beginning with 1974, Niekro would lead the league in innings pitched four times in six seasons, reaching a career-high of 342 innings in 1979.)

Niekro won fifteen games for a losing Braves' team in 1975, earning the second of his five All-Star nominations. On September 5 that year, the thirty-six-year-old was honored as the last active member of the original Atlanta Braves. At an age when most players begin to think about retirement, Niekro had just reached the midway point of what would be an incredible twenty-four-year major league career.

Phil Niekro (right) chats with his younger brother, Joe, before a 1979 game. That year the brothers became just the second siblings to each win twenty games in the same season.

Mr. Consistency

The 1976 Braves finished in last place, twenty-two games below .500 (70–92). Amazingly, Niekro had a record of 17–11, or six games *above* .500. In each of the next three seasons, he won more than twice as many games as any other pitcher on the Atlanta staff.

Niekro slumped to 16–20 in 1977 as the Braves compiled one of the worst records in franchise history (61–101). In addition to leading the league in losses, however, Niekro was also number one in games started, complete games, innings pitched, and strikeouts (a career-high 268). On the minus side, he also topped the circuit in walks and hits allowed.

Niekro's ability to pitch so many innings was a direct result of his reliance on the knuckleball. The wear and tear on his arm was minimal since the pitch required so little effort to throw. The unpredictability of the pitch, however, sometimes gave Niekro (and his catchers) nightmares. On July 29, 1977, he tied a major league record by striking out four Pittsburgh Pirate batters in a single inning (one batter got on base when a third strike could not be handled by the catcher). A little more than two years later, on August 4, 1979, he set two records in a contest against the Houston Astros by throwing four wild pitches in one inning and six in the game.

Later that year, at the age of forty, Niekro reached twenty wins for the third time in his career. His twentieth victory came against his brother Joe (the National League's only other twenty-game winner that season). The Niekro brothers became the second siblings in major-league history to win twenty in the same year. (In addition to his twenty-one wins, Phil also lost twenty games to become the first National League pitcher since 1905 to win and lose twenty in the same season.)

Still Going Strong

The Braves got back on the winning track in 1980, but Niekro led the league in losses for the fourth straight season. The next year, the players' strike limited him to a 7–7 record. With the Braves poised on the brink of respectability, the 1982 season got off to an ominous start. During spring training, Niekro was hit in the ribs by a batted ball from pitcher Rick Mahler. He began the regular season on the disabled list for the first time in his career.

Atlanta, meanwhile, got off to the fastest start in major league history by winning its first thirteen games. By the time Niekro returned to action in early May, the Braves were showing signs of contending for a division title for the first time in years. Niekro contributed more to the effort than anyone could have expected from a forty-three-year-old pitcher. He won an incredible seventeen of twenty-one decisions for the year, giving him a major-league-leading winning percentage of .810.

Niekro concentrates on a pitch during the 1983 season, the last he would play with the Braves. The 44-year-old pitcher proved that he was not ready to retire by winning 32 games over the next two seasons.

The Braves held on to edge the Los Angeles Dodgers for the National League West crown. They moved into the National League Championship Series against the St. Louis Cardinals, with Niekro given the honor of pitching the opener. He held a 1-0 lead in the fifth inning when rains caused the game to be postponed. He came back to start Game 2 of the series and left with a 3-2 lead after six innings. The Cardinals came back to win, however, and swept the Braves in three games to move on to the World Series.

The Braves were in contention again in 1983, as Niekro compiled an 11–10 mark. With the team looking toward the future, however, they decided to go with younger players. They did not offer him a contract after the season, and at age forty-four, he became a free agent.

Starting Over in a New League

After his release, Niekro was contacted by the St. Louis Cardinals, Oakland A's, Pittsburgh Pirates, and New York Yankees. On January 6, 1984, he signed a two-year contract with New York. He got off to a fast start with the Yankees, winning seven of his first nine decisions while moving to the top of the American League in earned run average. On July 4, he fanned five Texas Rangers in a Yankees win to make him the ninth pitcher in history to collect three thousand career strikeouts. Niekro made the American League All-Star team and went on to win sixteen games while losing only eight. His 3.09 earned run average was fourth-best in the league.

Niekro pitched one more season with the Yankees. He was their Opening Day starter on April 8, 1985, making him the second-oldest pitcher (at age forty-six) to ever start an opener. Although he was knocked out after only four innings, he proceeded to win sixteen games for New York. Niekro's final win came on October 6, the last day of the season. Pitching against the Toronto Blue Jays, he hurled a complete game, four-hit shutout for the three-hundredth win of his remarkable career. He was the eighteenth pitcher to reach that plateau, and the oldest pitcher ever to throw a shutout.

The Yankees released Niekro in late March 1986 and he signed with the Cleveland Indians a week later. In a year and

When the Braves established a Hall of Fame in 1990, Niekro (third from left) was one of the first players to be inducted, along with Hank Aaron, Eddie Mathews, and Warren Spahn.

a half with Cleveland and a half year with the Toronto Blue Jays, he added eighteen more wins to his total. On June 1, 1987, career win number 314 moved the Niekro brothers past Gaylord and Jim Perry into first place on the all-time brothers victory list.

After being released by Toronto, Niekro was invited back to Atlanta. He ended his career with a single appearance for the Braves on September 27, 1987. He lost to the San Francisco Giants and retired at the age of forty-eight after twenty-four major league seasons.

The Colorado Silver Bullets

After retiring as an active player, Niekro became a pitching instructor in the Braves organization. In 1991, he was hired as manager of Atlanta's Triple-A farm club in Richmond, Georgia. He remained in the position for only one year, however.

Having been a relentless competitor all his life, it was hard for him to accept the minor league philosophy in which player development is the most important thing. As he explained, "I found out it was too much for someone who left the clubhouse every night with winning or losing being the No. 1 thing. For me, that was very difficult."[26]

In 1994, Niekro accepted a job as manager of the Colorado Silver Bullets, a women's professional baseball team. He spent three years in the position, then took over as general manager in 1997. His experience with the team, which was forced to disband in 1998 due to lack of a sponsor, made him an enthusiastic proponent of the girls' game. "A lot of young ladies in this country want to play baseball," he said. "And they deserve the opportunity."[27]

Niekro was an excellent model for the women of the Silver Bullets. He ended his big-league career with 318 victories, good for fourteenth place on the all-time win list. He undoubtedly would have won even more had he pitched for a contending team for most of his career. Niekro had his uniform number retired by the Braves, and was elected to the Baseball Hall of Fame in Cooperstown, New York, in 1997.

Niekro currently lives with his wife in Flowery Branch, Georgia, where he closely follows his beloved Braves. He enjoyed all his years in the game he loves and would have changed only one thing. "If I could do everything over again," he said, "the only thing I would do differently is I would have played my entire career with Atlanta. I would not have worn another hat in my life."[28]

CHAPTER 4

Dale Murphy

D ale Murphy was the embodiment of the all-American boy. One of baseball's most durable players, he started out as a catcher and developed into one of the best outfielders in the league. He became the youngest player ever to win back-to-back Most Valuable Player awards in the National League. His strong religious beliefs and solid citizenship won him the respect of players and fans alike.

The Path to Greatness

Dale Bryan Murphy was born on March 12, 1956, the second child of Charles and Betty Murphy of Portland, Oregon. Charles was a sales representative for Westinghouse. Dale spent his formative years in Portland, except for a brief period when his father was transferred to Moraga, California. He was raised in a Presbyterian household where he was taught the Christian values that he would carry with him his entire life.

As a youngster, Dale enjoyed playing all sports, and did so with his parents' encouragement. He especially loved baseball, following in the footsteps of his great-grandfather (a semipro catcher) and his grandfather (a centerfielder in his youth).

Dale Murphy was one of Atlanta's greatest players, but it was his positive attitude, as much as his solid statistics, that made him a favorite of Braves fans.

When he was ten years old, Dale's parents enrolled him in the neighborhood Little League. Dale was not an immediate success, collecting just one hit his first season. He practiced whenever he could, however, and quickly improved.

At Woodrow Wilson High School in Portland, Dale played one year on the football team. It was as a catcher on coach Jack Dunn's baseball squad, however, that he made his mark. With his powerful arm, he gunned down runner after runner. As early as his junior year, Dunn thought the boy showed great potential, asking Dale's father, "Have you given any thought to your boy being a pro prospect?"[29]

The only thing that seemed to be holding Dale back was his hitting. By the time he was a senior, however, he began to fulfill his potential with the bat, hitting .400 that season while making the all-city and all-state teams.

Murphy had attracted the attention of scouts from every major-league team. Though some still had doubts about his hitting, others regarded him as the best catching prospect in the country. When the June 1974 draft came around, the Braves made him their number one pick and the fifth player taken overall. Although Murphy had signed a letter of intent to go to

Arizona State University, he decided the opportunity to play pro ball was too great to pass up. He signed with the Braves, but did not accept their first offer. "He told me it was too much money," recalled Braves' scouting supervisor Paul Snyder, "to take it back and reconsider. The offer was cut by $5,000."[30] It was one of the first indications the Braves had that Murphy was something special.

Problems Behind the Plate

Murphy began his pro career in 1974 with Kingsport of the Appalachian League. Over the next three years, he advanced through the Braves farm system to Greenwood, Savannah, and finally Richmond of the Triple-A International League. He was brought up to the major league club in September 1976 and made an impressive debut, going 2 for 4 with a pair of runs batted in in his first game.

Murphy spent a full season at Richmond in 1977, batting .305 with 22 home runs and a league-leading 90 runs batted in. He made another late-season appearance with the Braves, batting .316 in eighteen games.

By this time, however, Murphy had developed a mental block about throwing to second base. His throws occasionally hit the pitcher, but more often than not wound up in the outfield. (Trying to make light of the situation, his father told him, "One thing's for sure, Dale. Nobody will be stealing centerfield on you."[31])

Teammates and coaches were quick to offer advice, but nothing seemed to help. The more things he tried, the more confused he became. "I just couldn't throw accurately at all," he remembered. "It's kind of a hard thing to pinpoint exactly what you're feeling. It's frustrating not being able to throw a guy out. I didn't know what I was going to do."[32] His problem got so bad, at one point he even considered quitting the game.

The Solution

The Braves stuck with Murphy, however, and decided to try him at first base. He was the club's first baseman on Opening Day in 1978, and caught only twenty-one games all season. His throwing problems continued at his new position as well, and seemed to affect his performance at the plate. In that first full big-league season, he clouted 23 home runs and drove in 79 runs, but batted only .226. He also led the league in strikeouts with 145. Murphy showed some improvement the next year (he hit three home runs in a game against the Giants on May 18), but his problems in the field persisted.

It was not until the spring of 1980 that a solution presented itself. Atlanta manager Bobby Cox moved Murphy to the outfield and the change was dramatic. "By the middle of spring training that year," recalled Cox, "Murphy had become an adequate outfielder. And within a few months, he had become one of the best in the game."[33]

Murphy's career seemed to blossom with his move to the outfield. He opened the year in left field and proceeded to put together an All-Star season (his first of seven). Murphy clouted 33 home runs, drove home 89 runs, and scored 98 while raising his batting average to .281. He spent most of 1981 in center field, where his speed and strong arm were used to good advantage. Although the season was interrupted by a players' strike, he still managed to hit 21 home runs in only 104 games. His batting average, however, slumped to .247.

The Most Valuable Player

The Braves had struggled to a 50–56 record in the strike-shortened 1981 season, but were showing signs of promise. When Joe Torre was hired to replace Cox as manager for 1982, the club responded in spectacular fashion. Atlanta began the season by winning its first thirteen games to set a new major league record. Murphy led the team at bat and won Player of the Month honors for April.

The club cooled off after its sizzling start, but not Murphy. He finished the year with 36 home runs (second in the league) while tying for the league lead in runs batted in with 109. He also finished second in runs scored, third in total bases, and fourth in walks. In the field, he won the first of five straight Gold Glove awards for defensive excellence.

Murphy played in all 162 games as the Braves hung on to win the National League West. Unfortunately, he could not carry the team through the National League Championship

Murphy tracks down a fly ball in left field. After he was moved from first base before the 1980 season, Murphy developed into one of the game's best defensive outfielders.

Series. Playing against the St. Louis Cardinals, Murphy managed just three singles in eleven at bats as the Braves were defeated in three straight games.

For leading the club to its first postseason appearance since 1969, Murphy was voted the league's Most Valuable Player. In his typically modest manner, he downplayed the achievement. "I really owe the award to my teammates," he said. "If we hadn't won the division, I wouldn't have won the award."[34]

Murphy was not one to rest on his laurels. At Torre's request, he went to the Instructional League following the season (usually a venue for upcoming prospects) to work on his hitting. The results were impressive.

The Braves did not become division champs in 1983, but through no fault of Murphy's. He put together the finest season he would have in his eighteen major league years, reaching career highs in batting average (.302), runs scored (131), runs

Dale Murphy blasts a home run in a 1982 victory. Murphy was voted the league's Most Valuable Player in 1982, and he won the award again the following season.

batted in (a league-leading 121), and stolen bases (30). Having also hit 36 home runs, he became just the sixth 30-30 man (home runs and steals) in major league history. For good measure, he also led the league in slugging percentage.

Murphy was a runaway choice as the league's Most Valuable Player for the second consecutive season. He became just the fourth player in National League history to win the honor two years in a row, and at age twenty-seven, the youngest. The Braves finished in second place in the West with a record of 88–74. They would not finish with a winning record throughout the rest of Murphy's tenure with the team.

The Most Popular Brave

In addition to being the league's Most Valuable Player, Murphy was also the most popular Brave. He was well liked and respected by teammates and fans alike. As Bobby Cox said, "Murph gets as much respect as anyone I've ever known, because he lives his life the way we all wish we lived ours."[35]

Murphy's life centered on his family (he married Nancy Thomas, whom he met while attending Brigham Young University during the offseason, in 1979) and his religion. While playing for the Braves' Greenwood farm team in 1975, he became a Mormon, converting to the Church of Jesus Christ of Latter-day Saints. When his throwing problems arose, he seriously considered quitting baseball to do missionary work. "[Religion is] really important to me," he said. "But I decided it was best to stay in baseball. By so doing, I would be able to reach a lot of young people."[36]

Among the ways in which he reached young people was by donating his time to charities, visiting children in hospitals, and signing autographs for hours on end. Even more importantly, he became a positive role model through his behavior both on and off the field. Murphy didn't smoke, drink, chew tobacco, or curse. At the same time, he did not impose his values on others. "It's nice to be called the All-American boy," he admitted, "but guys have all kinds of images. I just try to live life the way that is right. I feel everybody has faults, though, and the name of the game is to improve yourself."[37]

The Best Player in the Game

Despite having won consecutive Most Valuable Player awards, Murphy was still able to improve himself in several areas in 1984. He either equaled or surpassed his season highs for doubles, triples, and home runs, hitting 36 home runs for the third year in a row. He also led the National League in slugging percentage and total bases. With slugging third baseman Bob Horner out for most of the year with a broken wrist, however, the Braves could finish no better than in a tie for second place in the West with a mark of 80–82.

Atlanta dropped to the bottom of the standings over the next couple of years, but Murphy continued to put up impressive numbers. By this time, he was receiving the recognition due one of the game's top performers. "He's the best I've ever seen," said Chicago Cubs pitching coach Billy Connors. "I've seen Murphy win games every way there is, a base hit in the ninth, a home run, a great catch, beating the throw to first on a double play. I've never seen anything like him before in my life."[38] Houston Astros catcher Alan Ashby simply said, "He's the best player in the game today."[39]

Murphy batted an even .300 in 1985, leading the league in home runs (37) and runs scored (118). He drove in 111 runs while collecting a career-high 185 base hits. Showing remarkable durability, he played in every one of the Braves' games for the fourth consecutive year. To cap off his season, he was named winner of the Lou Gehrig Award, presented annually to the major league player who best exemplifies the character of Lou Gehrig, both on and off the field.

On April 29, 1986, it appeared that Murphy's streak of 676 consecutive games would come to an end. After making a running catch of a fly ball in a game against the New York Mets, he cut his hand open on the fence at Atlanta–Fulton County Stadium. The cut required nine stitches to close and doctors said Murphy would be out of action for at least a week. The next day, however, he came off the bench to pinch hit in the fifth inning. In one of the most dramatic moments in team history, Murphy slugged a home run off New York's Dwight Gooden. He was back in the starting lineup the next day and continued to play until being given a day off in early July. His streak of 740 consecutive games was the twelfth-longest in major league history.

One Final Monster Year

Murphy's production dropped off in 1986, in part due to his finger injury and other physical woes. "He played hurt all season," said manager Chuck Tanner. "The injuries had a great effect on his season. His hands were a mess. . . . He was like a prizefighter who's had his hands all banged up."[40]

Murphy vowed to bounce back and did so with another MVP-caliber season in 1987. Tanner named him team captain in spring training, and moved him to right field, in part to take better advantage of his strong throwing arm and to reduce the wear and tear on his legs. Murphy responded by batting .295 for the fifth-place Braves, and stroking a career-high 44 home runs. He drove in 105 runs and scored 115, reaching the triple-digit mark in both categories for the last time in his career.

The next year, Murphy's batting average dipped nearly seventy points to .226. Although he continued to be a solid run producer, driving home 77 runs, it was obvious that time was beginning to catch up with him. Off the field, however, he showed no sign of slowing down his good works. He was presented with the Roberto Clemente Award, given annually to the player who best exemplifies the game of baseball, sportsmanship, community involvement, and contribution to his team.

Murphy underwent arthroscopic surgery on his right knee after the season. He came back to lead the Braves in runs batted in for the eighth straight year in 1989, producing one final glorious moment on July 27. On that day, he slugged a pair of three-run home runs in the sixth inning of a game against the San Francisco Giants to tie the major-league records for home runs and RBIs in a single inning.

The End of a Long Association

Murphy returned to the Braves for his fifteenth season in 1990. The years had taken their toll on his body and at the age of thirty-four, he was clearly on the downside of his career. On

August 4, Atlanta traded him to the Philadelphia Phillies, along with pitcher Tommy Greene, in exchange for Jeff Parrett, Jim Vatcher, and Victor Rosario. Murphy tried to look at the trade from a positive viewpoint. "I feel like I haven't produced like I feel I can in recent years," he said at a press conference. "Maybe with a new direction, I feel I can play a few more years."[41]

The response to the trade in Atlanta was one of anger. The newspapers were flooded with letters from fans who promised to never attend another Braves' game. Even the players were unhappy. "You'd think I'd be happy because I get to play every day with Murphy gone," said his replacement, David Justice. "But I'm miserable. He meant so much to me. It feels strange without him."[42]

Philadelphia general manager Lee Thomas felt Murphy still had much to contribute to his new team. "He's a good defensive outfielder," said Thomas, "and he still has all of his hitting capabilities."[43] Murphy stroked 18 home runs and drove home 81 runs for the Phillies in 1991, but was limited to eighteen games the next year due to knee problems. He was released by Philadelphia in April 1992 and signed with the expansion Colorado Rockies. After hitting just .143 for Colorado in 42 at bats, Murphy hung up his spikes on May 27, 1993.

Murphy's Mission

Since retiring from baseball, Murphy has devoted his life to his family and his church. He taught religious school in Roswell, Georgia, then served as the leader of a congregation in Utah. In 1997, Murphy moved to Boston where he served a three-year term as president of the Boston mission for the Church of Jesus Christ of Latter-day Saints. In that role, he was in charge of overseeing the training and work of young missionaries throughout New England. "It was intense," recalled Murphy. "It's like you have 180 children that you are constantly worried about. Your stomach is kind of always churning."[44]

After leaving his position in Boston, Murphy moved with his wife and eight children back to Alpine, Utah. His popularity in the state has caused him to consider becoming involved in politics, possibly as a future governor of the state. "It's kind of someone else's idea," he said. "It's the people that asked me.

Murphy kneels on second base after hitting a double in a 1990 game. He would finish his career with 2,111 hits and 398 home runs.

... I'm interested, but a lot of things have to happen."[45]

No matter how successful he is in politics, Murphy will always be remembered as one of the best players ever to wear an Atlanta uniform. Murphy finished his career with a lifetime batting average of .265. He hit 398 homers and drove home 1,266 runs. On June 13, 1994, his uniform number was retired by the Braves. As great as he was as a player, however, he was an even better person. In the words of former teammate Phil Niekro, "People keep looking for words to describe him. Well, there aren't enough good words or words good enough."[46]

CHAPTER 5

Tom Glavine

Tom Glavine is arguably the best all-around athlete among modern-day pitchers. He has won twenty games in a season five times in a career that has seen him post more than 250 victories. He is also an outstanding fielder and one of the best-hitting pitchers around.

A Love of Sports

Thomas Michael Glavine was born on March 25, 1966, in Concord, Massachusetts. He was one of four children (three boys and a girl) born to Fred and Millie Glavine. His father owned a construction business in Billerica, the suburb of Boston in which Tom grew up.

Being raised in New England, Tom's first love was hockey. He began to skate when he was just four years old and played in a local league shortly after. When he was seven, he was introduced to Little League baseball. His parents encouraged his interest in sports, but made sure he had his priorities straight. "Dad's rule," he recalled, "was that before I did anything else after school, I had to get my homework done."[47]

Tom's talent showed through at an early age. "He's one of those kids who was always playing each level of sports at the earliest age," remembered his father. "He was just an athlete, good enough so the older kids would let him play. He was always the youngest."[48]

Hockey or Baseball?

Tom played close to one hundred games a year in Billerica Youth Hockey and his skills developed rapidly. Playing center on the Billerica Memorial High School squad, he was good enough to be selected to the *Boston Globe* All-Scholastic team twice. As a senior, he led Eastern Massachusetts in scoring and was named the Merrimack Valley Conference Most Valuable Player. Tom's style was efficient in a quiet sort of way. "Not the flashiest kid on the ice," said his father, "but at the end of the game you'd look at the stat sheet and he'd done most of the scoring."[49]

Tom Glavine fires a pitch during a 2002 contest. Glavine won 242 games for the Braves between 1987 and 2002.

Tom was scouted by many National Hockey League teams. When it came time for the league's annual draft, he was the sixty-ninth player taken in 1984, selected by the Los Angeles Kings in the fourth round. He was taken before such future NHL stars as Brett Hull and Luc Robitaille.

Glavine's decision whether or not to sign with the Kings was made more difficult by the fact that he was also being recruited by several colleges. "I had a full hockey scholarship to the University of Lowell," he recalled. "That was a big thing. Four years of college for free."[50]

By this time, Glavine had also developed into an excellent baseball player. He pitched and played first base and the outfield for coach John Sidorovich's Billerica squad. The finest moment of Glavine's high school career came at the end of his junior year. Playing against Brockton High School in the state championship game, he pitched nine scoreless innings and came out with the game tied, 0-0. He moved to center field and threw out the potential winning run at the plate in the eleventh inning. To cap off his day, he singled to lead off the thirteenth inning and eventually came around to score the winning run. He was named Player of the Year by the *Boston Globe* and attracted the attention of numerous big-league scouts.

Five days before the National Hockey League draft, the Braves selected Glavine in the second round of the baseball amateur draft. Although disappointed that he hadn't been selected by the hometown Red Sox, Glavine was flattered to be picked so high by Atlanta. Believing his prospects for a long career to be better in baseball than in hockey, he signed a contract with the Braves calling for an $80,000 bonus.

A Fast Trip Through the Minors

The six-foot one-inch, 185-pound left-hander was assigned to Bradenton, the Braves' rookie farm team in the Gulf Coast League. Although he won only two of five decisions there, he impressed everyone with his live fastball, striking out thirty-four batters in only thirty-two innings and compiling a 3.34 earned run average. The following year, he was moved up to Sumter of the Class A South Atlantic League.

Even though Glavine had been successful using just a fast-ball and curve, he realized he had to develop a third pitch. "I knew as I moved up the ladder my success wouldn't continue unless I started throwing a change-up," he said, "so I started tinkering with a circle change-up that is thrown with your thumb on the bottom of the ball and index finger over the ball and the rest of the fingers around the ball in the form of a circle. That worked."[51] He proceeded to have a solid season, leading the league in earned run average while compiling a 9–6 record and 174 strikeouts in 169 innings.

Glavine started 1986 with Greenville of the Double-A Southern League. He was 11-6 when he was promoted to Atlanta's top farm team, the Richmond Braves of the Triple-A International League. There, he struggled for the first time in his pro career, winning just one of his seven starts and losing five. Glavine went to the Instructional League after the season to work on his mechanics. The next spring he was invited to the major league camp.

The Braves wanted Glavine to play a full season of Triple-A ball, so he again reported to Richmond in 1987. Although he was only 6–12, he pitched better than his record indicated, compiling a 3.35 earned run average for a weak team. Following a loss to the Toledo Mud Hens on August 12, he was told he was being called up to the big-league club.

A Slow Start

The Braves team that Glavine joined was in the midst of a fourth consecutive losing season. Anxious to see what his new young left-hander could do, manager Chuck Tanner inserted Glavine into the starting rotation. In his debut against the Houston Astros on August 17, Glavine lasted just three and two-thirds innings, surrendering 10 hits and 6 earned runs. He took the loss, but bounced back to record his first major-league win five days later against the Pittsburgh Pirates. He won one more game that season to give him a 2–4 mark in his first taste of big-league action.

The 1988 Braves team was one of the worst in the franchise's history. Partly because of that, the club stayed with Glavine despite his early struggles. At twenty-one years of age, he posted a 7–17 record, leading the National League in losses. He

Glavine progressed quickly through the minor leagues but had some trouble after joining the Braves late in 1987. In nine starts, he posted a 2–4 record with a 5.51 earned run average.

pitched better than his record indicated, however, since the club had a porous defense and did not score a lot of runs.

The Turning Point

During spring training the next year, Glavine experimented with a new grip for his change-up. He had picked up a ball during batting practice and held it in an unusual way. When he threw it back to the infield, it felt natural coming out of his

hand. He tried the grip the next time he pitched
results.

The pitch improved Glavine's performance dr̶̶̶ ̶̶̶̶̶̶̶̶̶̶̶̶̶̶̶̶̶.̶ As
he relates in his autobiography, "The key with my new pitch
was I didn't have to slow down my arm speed or change anything with my delivery. Everything was the same. You want to
be able to stand on the mound and say to the hitter, 'I'm throwing a change-up!' but when it comes out of my hand it looks
just like a fastball to the hitter."[52]

Glavine put his new pitch to good use and fashioned a 14–8
record in 1989. His 3.68 earned run average was nearly a full
run better than the previous year. The following season, however, he dropped back to 10–12. The problem, he later said, was
more mental than physical: he simply did not employ his
change-up often enough. He learned his lesson well, however.
With the Braves having added some good young talent to their
roster, both Glavine and the team were ready for a break-
through year in 1991.

A Magical Season

In an effort to turn things around, the Braves hired John
Schuerholz as their new general manager following their third
consecutive last place finish in 1990. Schuerholz immediately
began trying to instill a new attitude in the team, especially
among the younger players who had known nothing but losing in their short big-league careers. He also added several important players, including first baseman Sid Bream, second
baseman Rafael Belliard, third baseman Terry Pendleton, and
outfielder Deion Sanders.

With an improved defense behind him, Glavine began the
1991 season by winning his first six decisions. His confidence
improved with each good outing and the wins began piling up.
By the All-Star break, he had a 12–4 record with a 1.98 earned
run average. He was selected by manager Lou Piniella to start
the All-Star classic for the National League and pitched two
scoreless innings in the contest.

The Braves were one game below .500 at midseason (39–40).
In the second half of the season, the club showed significant
improvement. By the end of August they were in the thick of

the National League West divisional race. Everything seemed to go Atlanta's way as the Braves overtook the Dodgers to win the division title by a game in the last weekend of the season. Glavine finished with a record of 20-11. He tied for the league lead in wins and complete games, while his 2.55 earned run average was third-lowest in the circuit. Following the end of the season, he became the second Braves' pitcher to win the Cy Young Award (Warren Spahn was the first in 1957).

In the National League Championship Series against Pittsburgh, Glavine lost two games, including a 1-0 shutout in Game 5. The Braves still managed to upset the Pirates in seven games to move into the World Series against the Minnesota Twins. There, Atlanta's fairytale season finally came to an end. The Twins defeated the Braves in seven games. Glavine lost Game 2 by a score of 3-2, but bounced back to take Game 5 for his first postseason victory.

Repeat Success

Glavine and the Braves repeated their success in 1992. He again won twenty games while leading the league in shutouts with five and posting a 2.76 ERA for the pennant-winning team. Glavine finished second in the Cy Young voting to Chicago Cubs pitcher—and future Braves teammate—Greg Maddux (who would also win the award in each of the next three seasons).

Glavine was hit hard by the Pirates in the National League Championship Series, losing games three and six. He bounced back, however, in the World Series against the Toronto Blue Jays. He hurled a four-hitter to win the opener, 3-1, then lost Game 4, 2-1.

The Braves signed Maddux as a free agent following the season, giving Atlanta the top pitching duo in the league. The competition between Glavine and Maddux and the team's other starters brought out the best in each. "We all want each other to do well," said Glavine. "And we all want to do better than the last guy. No question, we all want to outdo each other."[53] Maddux and Glavine combined for forty-two wins in 1993, then twenty-nine more in the strike-shortened 1994 season. That year, Glavine assumed a new role with the team.

Glavine's Other Side

Glavine had always been interested in details of the collective bargaining agreement that had been agreed upon by the owners and players. When Dale Murphy gave up his position as the Braves' player representative in 1991, Glavine took over the job. Two years later, he was elected assistant National League player representative. "I don't know how he got that deeply involved," said his father. "I guess it was because he was brought up always to stand up for what he believed in."[54]

When the players went out on strike in 1994, Glavine was one of the key spokesmen for the players' association as a member of the negotiating committee. As such, he was given a great deal of criticism from many of the fans in Atlanta (a non-union city) who sided with the owners. As Braves president Stan Kasten explained, "He became a symbol in this market for a lot of the things people are unhappy with."[55]

When the strike eventually ended the next year, Glavine was concerned about the fans' reaction. He was strongly booed at the outset of the season, but as the year progressed, the booing subsided. He finished with a record of 16–7 as the Braves dominated the National League East. Atlanta defeated the Colorado Rockies in four games in the National League Division Series, then swept the Cincinnati Reds in a four-game National League Championship Series. Glavine pitched well in the two series, but came away without a decision. He saved his best for the World Series.

A Magnificent Performance Under Pressure

The Braves' opponent in the World Series was the Cleveland Indians. Atlanta was anxious to atone for its losses in the 1991 and 1992 Series. Maddux started Game 1 and gave the Braves the lead with a two-hit, 3-2 victory. Glavine followed him in Game 2 and defeated the Indians, 4-3. Cleveland, however, refused to give up. They won two of the next three games and returned to Atlanta for Game 6 down three games to two.

With a chance to clinch the World Series, Glavine got the call to start. In the ultimate pressure situation for a ballplayer, his attention was entirely on the task at hand. As Maddux recalled, "Tom was completely focused, locked in. There could have been people standing a foot behind him heckling and he wouldn't have heard them."[56]

Glavine totally dominated a Cleveland team that had one of the best lineups in the majors. He did not allow a single base hit until Tony Pena blooped a single to right field in the top half of the sixth inning. When the Braves came to bat in the bottom half of the inning, the outcome of the game was still in doubt. Atlanta had squandered several scoring opportunities and the score stood at 0-0. That changed, however, when outfielder Dave Justice led off with a home run to deep right field.

Glavine held the Indians in check without another hit in the seventh and eighth innings, but was beginning to tire. Relief pitcher Mark Wohlers came into the game and retired Cleveland in the ninth inning. After two near-misses over the previous three years, the Braves were finally world champions.

In pitching the game of his life, Glavine pitched eight innings with only one hit ball. For the Series, he won two games while giving up just four hits and two runs in fourteen innings of work (a 1.29 earned run average). Glavine was named the Series Most Valuable Player as the city of Atlanta celebrated its first championship in any major sport.

A Well-Deserved Reputation

Following their victory over the Indians, the Braves won the Eastern Division crown in each of the next seven years. Over that span, Glavine averaged nearly seventeen wins per season. He reached the twenty-win mark two times, notching twenty victories in 1998 and twenty-one in 2000. He recorded a career-best 2.47 earned run average in 1998 when he won his second Cy Young Award. Unfortunately, despite their amazing success in the regular season, the Braves could not win another World Series. They won pennants in 1996 and 1999, but were stopped by the New York Yankees in the Fall Classic both times.

Throughout the decade of the nineties, Glavine established himself as one of the smartest pitchers in the game. Instead of relying on an overpowering fastball, his strength has been his mental toughness and control. "He's got command of four pitches," said Atlanta pitching coach Leo Mazzone, "the fast-ball, curveball, slider, and change. He has great control, and he can change speeds as well as anyone in this game."[57]

Because Glavine's pitches were always around the plate, umpires were often accused of calling strikes on pitches that actually missed the corners. In 1999, the strike zone was redefined and umpires were instructed to call such pitches more carefully. Glavine and Maddux were expected to be the two pitchers most affected by the new strike zone.

Glavine struggled through the first half of the year. "I didn't handle it well," he recalled. "I went out there anticipating changes rather than reacting to them. I wound up creating problems for myself."[58] He adjusted, however, and finished the year with a 14–11 record. The next year, he experimented with

---

Glavine pitched eight shutout innings, giving up only one hit, in the crucial sixth game of the 1995 World Series. Atlanta's 1-0 victory gave the Braves franchise its first championship since the 1966 move from Milwaukee.

several new pitches. The result was a 21–9 record and a second-place finish in the Cy Young voting.

A New Start

Glavine's record over the years earned him a salary in line with his performance. He signed a $42 million, five-year contract that made him one of the highest-paid pitchers in the game. Following the 2002 season, at age thirty-six, he became a free agent. With 242 career victories to his credit, Glavine wanted to sign a multi-year deal that would assure him a chance at making a run at 300 wins. The Braves, however, were hesitant to make such a long-term commitment to a pitcher his age. They eventually offered him a three-year contract, which he turned down.

The Philadelphia Phillies and New York Mets also had been bidding for his services, but most observers felt he would ultimately re-sign with Atlanta. After several weeks of contract

Glavine argues with an umpire about a close call. The Atlanta ace's control enabled him to win a second Cy Young Award in 1998, but he was frustrated when umpires changed the way they called balls and strikes in 1999.

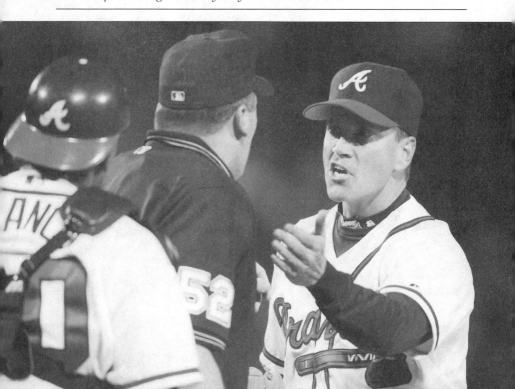

After the 2002 season, Glavine became a free agent. He ultimately signed a contract with the New York Mets and was the team's starter on Opening Day 2003.

talks, however, Glavine decided to sign with the Mets, who offered him a $35 million three-year deal, with an option for a fourth. "It's almost surreal that it happened," said Glavine. "I never thought I would play for someone else. I thought I would play my whole career with the Braves. I held out hope that things would work out, but they didn't. There's a lot of emotions. It's a tough time."[59] His sixteen-year career with the Braves officially came to an end.

In his first sixteen big-league seasons, Glavine collected 242 wins, leaving him just 58 shy of the magic 300 mark. He compiled a 3.37 earned run average to go along with his five twenty-win seasons. Glavine added twelve more wins in postseason play, and compiled a 2.16 earned run average in fifty-eight and one-third innings of World Series action. The fact that he led National League pitchers in games started on six occasions, including four straight years from 1999 to 2002, is testimony to his consistency and durability. One of the top winners in the decade of the nineties, he will receive serious consideration for the Hall of Fame when he becomes eligible at some future date.

In the meantime, Glavine enjoys spending his free time with his wife and children. He is an avid golfer and often helps raise money by playing in celebrity golf tournaments. Glavine is very active in the Atlanta community and gives much of his time to charities including the Leukemia Society of America, the Georgia Counsel on Child Abuse, the Georgia Transplant Foundation, the Juvenile Diabetes Foundation, and the National Hemophilia Foundation.

CHAPTER 6

Greg Maddux

One of the premier pitchers in the game today, Greg Maddux has won a National League–record four Cy Young awards. He is one of the great control pitchers of all time, and one of only two men to have won fifteen or more games in fifteen consecutive seasons. He is also an outstanding fielder with thirteen Gold Gloves to his credit.

A Sports-Minded Family

Gregory Alan Maddux was born in San Angelo, Texas, on April 14, 1966. His parents, David and Linda, also had two older children, a son Mike (who also became a major-league baseball player) and a daughter, Teri. David was in the Air Force which meant he traveled around a lot. Over the years, the Maddux family lived in Texas, Indiana, North Dakota, California, and Madrid, Spain. When Greg was ten years old, his father was transferred to Las Vegas, Nevada, where he spent the last three years of his military career. After leaving the Air Force, he became a poker dealer in a local casino. His wife worked as a dispatcher for the Henderson County police department.

71

In 2002, Atlanta's Greg Maddux tied a major-league record by recording 15 or more victories in 15 consecutive seasons.

All the Maddux children were involved in sports. "It consumed most of our time," remembered Linda, "because there was always one child on a playing field someplace. Dave coached, and I baked cookies and cupcakes for fund-raisers and after-game snacks and that sort of thing."[60]

Baseball was Greg's sport of choice and he demonstrated an aptitude for it right from the beginning. As his father recalled, "He was always so far ahead of anybody else he played, especially his own age-group. Continuously, since the time he could walk, he always played with Mike, and he was as good as most boys four years older or so. In some cases, he was better."[61]

At the age of six, Greg was eligible to play tee-ball. Since he was so far advanced for his age, his father tried to get permission for him to play in the next highest level (peewee ball). At first, David's request was denied. However, when he volunteered to coach a team if Greg was allowed to play on it, the decision was reversed. Greg quickly proved to be the best player on the team.

Following in His Brother's Footsteps

When Greg was eleven, his older brother Mike began attending informal practices held by Rusty Medar, a former big-league scout who followed the city's best players. Medar's goal was to develop young players in the area. Greg eventually got Medar's attention. "After about three or four weeks," remembered Mike, "I said to Mr. Medar, 'Put Greg out there. Let him play.'. . . The first time Greg threw, Mr. Medar said, 'I don't know where the boy got those mechanics, but let me tell you this: Don't you let anybody change those mechanics. He's going to be something.'"[62]

Medar began to teach the youngster some of the finer points of pitching. He showed him how to throw a fastball which dipped away from left-hand hitters. He also taught him the change-up, which would eventually become his most effective pitch.

At Valley High School in Las Vegas, Greg did not need the change-up. His fastball, though not overpowering, was good enough to get out most high school batters. The five-foot eleven-inch, 150-pounder honed his talents under the tutelage of coach Rodger Fairless.

Mike was drafted by the Philadelphia Phillies when Greg was a junior. Greg compiled an 8–1 record that year and went 8–2 as a senior, winning all-state honors both years and impressing his coach with his attitude. "When it was time to play," recalled Fairless, "Greg was always there—very serious, very competitive and very tough. You wouldn't want to pick a fight with him when he was pitching whereas away from the game he probably couldn't lick a soul."[63]

Although Greg had dominated his high school competition, many major-league scouts thought he was too small to overpower professional hitters. The Chicago Cubs finally selected him in the second round of the 1984 amateur draft, the thirty-first overall pick. By this time, Greg had been offered a scholarship from the University of Arizona, which had one of the best collegiate baseball programs in the country. Carefully weighing his options, he decided he would have a better chance of making it to the big leagues if he began his pro career right away. He signed with Chicago for an $85,000 bonus and promised his parents he would not touch the money until he made the major leagues. The Cubs assigned him to their Pikeville farm club in the Appalachian League where he began his pro career in 1984.

The Road to the Majors

Maddux gave a good account of himself in his first pro season, winning six games while losing three for Pikeville. He had an earned run average of just 2.63 and tied for the league lead in shutouts with two. The following year, he was promoted to Peoria of the Midwest League. There, he finished among the league leaders with thirteen wins and made the All-Star team.

In 1986, Maddux began the year with Pittsfield, but spent most of the season with the Cubs' top farm team at Iowa in the

Greg Maddux was just 20 years old when he pitched in his first major-league game, in 1986. During his time with the Chicago Cubs, Maddux proved he was a tough competitor.

Class AAA American Association. He continued to impress those who saw him play, compiling a 10–1 record with a 3.02 earned run average. He was rewarded for his stellar work with a call-up to the major league team on September 1 when the rosters were expanded from twenty-five players to forty.

Maddux's boyish appearance and less-than-impressive physique caught Chicago manager Gene Michael by surprise. Recalled Michael, "I was standing in front of the dugout with one of my coaches, John Vuckovich. And Vuckovich says to me, 'Aren't you going to say hello to your new pitcher?' I said, 'Where is he?' Vuckovich points into the dugout and says, 'Right there.' I say, 'I don't see anybody.' And he says, 'Right in front of you, in the dugout.' And I say, 'That's the batboy.' And he says, '*That's* your new pitcher.'"[64]

The very next day, Maddux made his major league debut against the Houston Astros. He entered the 6-6 game in the eighteenth inning and surrendered a home run to take the loss. At age twenty, he became the youngest player to appear in a game for the Cubs in nineteen years.

Maddux's first big-league start came five days later. He pitched a complete game victory as the Cubs defeated the Cincinnati Reds, 11-3. He won his second game later that month in a contest that had historic implications. When he defeated the Philadelphia Phillies on September 29, his pitching opponent was his brother, Mike. The game marked the first matchup of rookie brothers in major league history. Greg finished the year with a record of 2–4 and an earned run average of 5.52.

Mad Dog Maddux

In 1987, Maddux came out of spring training as the Cub's fifth starter. Unfortunately, he began to exhibit behavior that troubled the team. Always an intense competitor, he began to get angry about every little thing. He would yell obscenities at himself on the mound if a pitch did not go where he wanted it, or argue with an umpire over a close call. It got to the point where his teammates began calling him "Mad Dog."

Also like many young pitchers, Maddux tried to get by mainly using his fastball. Although that strategy worked in the minors, big-league hitters soon caught up with him. By the middle of the season, his record had fallen to 6–10, causing Chicago to return him to the minors.

After winning three games with Iowa, Maddux was recalled to the big-league club. He remained with the team for the rest of the year but lost his last six decisions as he continued to struggle. He finished the year with a record of 6–14 and a 5.52 earned run average.

That winter, Maddux went to Venezuela to play winter ball with the team representing the city of Maracaibo in the Venezuelan League. Cubs' pitching coach Dick Pole went along to help him work on developing an off-speed pitch and to change his attitude. Maddux improved both and headed into the 1988 season a changed pitcher.

The New Maddux

The change in Maddux was apparent in his very first start of 1988. Pitching against the Braves, he allowed just three hits to defeat Atlanta by a score of 3-0. His dramatic improvement continued through the first half of the year. By the end of May, his record stood at 8–3. Included was a stretch in which he did not allow an earned run in twenty-six and two-thirds consecutive innings.

Maddux did not lose a game in June and was pitching as well as anyone in baseball. His work drew the attention of everyone in the game, including St. Louis Cardinals manager Whitey Herzog, who selected Maddux as one of the pitchers for the National League All-Star team. At the age of twenty-two, he became the youngest Cub ever to earn that honor.

Maddux's record was 15–3 at the break. He tailed off after the All-Star Game, but still finished with eighteen wins (fifth in the league) and an earned run average of 3.18. He pitched 249 innings (also fifth in the league) and had nine complete games. Maddux's performance showed everyone that he was on the brink of stardom.

The Best Pitcher in the League

The Cubs won the National League East division title in 1989 with just their second winning season since 1972. Maddux was one of the main reasons for the team's success. He won nineteen games and lost only twelve while lowering his earned run average to 2.95. In the balloting for the Cy Young Award, Maddux finished third.

Maddux struggled in his first taste of postseason action. He was hit hard by the San Francisco Giants in games one and four of the National League Championship Series (NLCS). The Giants defeated Chicago in five games to end the Cubs' season and send them home with high hopes for 1990.

Unfortunately, Chicago fell to fourth place the next year despite another solid performance by Maddux. He won fifteen games while finishing second in the league in innings pitched and fourth in complete games. In addition, he won the first of his thirteen Gold Glove awards for fielding excellence. With regards to his fielding, first baseman Mark Grace commented,

Maddux swings at an offering from another pitcher. The Atlanta ace has often helped his cause at the plate: He has more than 215 career hits.

"He's the best I've every played with, as far as getting over to first base."[65]

Maddux continued to shine in 1991, again winning fifteen games while leading the league in both starts and innings pitched. With his contract up after the season, he approached the Cubs about signing a long-term deal that would assure his future. Having won sixty-seven games over the previous four seasons (best in the National League), Maddux was looking for a four- or five-year contract worth in the neighborhood of $5 million per year.

After winning the 1992 Cy Young Award for the Cubs, Maddux decided to become a free agent. He justified the Braves' $28 million investment in 1993 by winning his second Cy Young Award with a 20–10 record and a 2.36 ERA.

The Cubs, however, were in no rush to make such a commit-
ment. They knew Maddux could not become a free agent for
another year. They offered him a one-year deal worth $4.2 mil-
lion, which he accepted.

The following year, Maddux entered the ranks of the pitching elite. Leading a team that finished in fourth place with a
record of 78–84, he won twenty games for the first time in his
career to tie for the league lead. He also topped the circuit in innings pitched, and finished third in both earned run average
(2.18) and strikeouts (199). For his efforts, he won the first of his
four Cy Young Awards as the outstanding pitcher in the
league.

Chicago was showing no sign of becoming a pennant contender in the immediate future. The team offered Maddux a
new five-year contract worth $27.5 million, but by this time
money was no longer the only factor. Maddux wanted to pitch
in a World Series. He decided to become a free agent in hopes
of signing with a team that would give him the chance to fulfill
that dream.

Atlanta Beckons

The New York Yankees were one of the clubs that expressed interest in signing Maddux. Never hesitant to spend money when
going after a player they desired, the New Yorkers stunned him
with an incredible $37.5 million, six-year deal—$10 million
more than what the Cubs had offered. The money was tempt-
ing, but Maddux was not sure the situation was best for him.
He preferred to remain in the National League, where he was
already familiar with all the hitters. In addition, the Yankees
were still a player or two away from being a title contender.

Shortly after receiving the Yankees offer, Maddux was contacted by the Braves. Atlanta offered him a five-year deal worth
$28 million. Maddux had always enjoyed the city of Atlanta. In
addition, he liked the idea of being one of several stars on a
strong pitching staff rather than the one expected to carry a
team on his shoulders. After discussing his options with his
wife, he finally accepted the Braves' proposal, shocking most of
baseball by turning down the higher offer. He signed with
Atlanta in early December.

Maddux began his stay in Atlanta by picking up where he left off in Chicago. In his very first year (1993), he compiled a 20–10 record while leading the league with a 2.36 earned run average. He also topped the circuit in complete games and innings pitched to earn his second consecutive Cy Young Award. Atlanta led the majors with 104 wins, but lost to the Philadelphia Phillies in six games in the NLCS. Maddux earned his first postseason victory in Game 2, but took the loss in the final contest after being struck by a line drive off the bat of Philadelphia second baseman Mickey Morandini.

The players' strike brought the 1994 season to an early end, preventing Maddux from recording his third straight twenty-win year. He did win sixteen games while leading the majors in earned run average. His incredible 1.56 mark was 1.09 runs ahead of the second-best pitcher, setting a major league record. Despite making only twenty-five starts, he also set a career high by hurling ten complete games. His performance helped him become the first pitcher in history to win three consecutive Cy Young awards. Although the personal honors were nice, the thing he desired most—a World Series ring—still eluded him.

Champions at Last

Maddux was magnificent again in 1995. He was an amazing 19–2 for the year with a brilliant 1.63 league-leading earned run average that made him the first pitcher since Walter Johnson in 1918–19 to have an ERA under 1.80 in consecutive seasons. Demonstrating uncanny control, he walked just twenty-three batters the entire season and had a streak of fifty-one consecutive innings without allowing a walk. For the second straight year, Maddux was the unanimous winner of the National League Cy Young Award, giving him four in a row overall.

The Braves again won the National League East (they had switched divisions the previous year). They then defeated the Colorado Rockies in the League Division Series and the Cincinnati Reds in the NLCS to reach the World Series. Their opponents were the powerful Cleveland Indians.

Maddux took the mound for the Braves in Game 1. In his first taste of Series action, he dominated the Indians, tossing a

An Atlanta crowd cheers Maddux as he walks off the field. Throughout his career, Maddux has relied on pinpoint control and an understanding of hitters to dominate opposing teams.

two-hitter for a 3-2 win. He later called the game his best ever. With the Braves up, three games to one, Maddux started Game 5 in Cleveland with a chance to clinch the championship. The Indians managed to beat him, 5-4, however, to send the Series back to Atlanta. There, Tom Glavine pitched a masterful one-hitter to give Atlanta the victory. The Braves were at the top of the baseball world and Maddux finally earned his championship ring.

Consistency and Excellence

Following their Series win, the Braves finished first in the National League East in each of the next seven seasons. They made it back to the Series in 1996 and 1999, but could not get past the Yankees either year. Throughout their incredible run, Maddux has been a model of consistency. He won at least fifteen games each year (including nineteen three times) to give him a streak of fifteen consecutive years with fifteen or more wins. Only one other pitcher—the immortal Cy Young—has accomplished that feat.

In addition to having led the National League in wins three times, Maddux has also led in earned run average four times, complete games three times, and innings pitched and shutouts five times each. He has won thirteen consecutive Gold Glove awards, been named to the All-Star team eight times, and won eleven games in the postseason. As of the start of the 2003 season, he had 273 career wins, putting him on track to reach the magic 300 number before he is forty years old.

Maddux has accomplished all this despite the fact that he is not a power pitcher. His control, intelligence, and knowledge of opposing hitters are second to none. "He doesn't have the best fastball in baseball," says Braves announcer Skip Caray. "You don't gasp like you did when Gibson and Koufax pitched. He doesn't have the best curveball. But he does have the best control in baseball, and I think he knows more about pitching."[66]

Off the field, Maddux prefers to stay out of the spotlight. He spends most of his time with his family. In an effort to give something back to his community, he established the Greg Maddux Foundation together with his wife, Kathy. "We put some of our money into it," said Kathy, "plus money Greg receives from appearances. And we use it to support children's homes, domestic crisis shelters for battered women, and boys and girls clubs."[67]

Maddux is the best right-handed pitcher of his generation and one of the best of all time. After he retires, he will certainly join the immortals of the game in the Baseball Hall of Fame in Cooperstown, New York. Until then, he continues to baffle batters in his quest to bring the Braves another world championship.

CHAPTER 7

Chipper Jones

Switch-hitter Chipper Jones is one of the best all-around young hitters in the game today. He has averaged over 30 home runs and 100 runs batted in for each of his eight full major league seasons, while batting at a .309 clip. He has been a vital cog in the powerful Braves teams of the last decade, and was the National League's Most Valuable Player in 1999.

Growing Up with Baseball

Larry Wayne Jones Jr. is the only child of Larry and Lynn Jones of DeLand, Florida. He was born on April 24, 1972, and grew up in the small town of Pierson (population 2,988), known as the Fern Capital of the World. As a child, Larry was so much like his father that everyone started calling him Chipper, short for "chip off the old block." "Chipper is a good name," says Jones. "If I was called Larry Jones, who'd remember that? Chipper is one of those first names people remember."[68]

Chipper grew up loving all sports, but especially baseball. His father was an algebra teacher and baseball coach at Taylor High School in Pierson. Chipper was introduced to the game at the age of three when he began going with his dad to practices.

He was so small he could not hold a regular size bat, so his father made him one from a piece of PVC pipe. By the time he was five, he was already learning how to hit from both sides of the plate.

Right from the beginning, Chipper displayed an affinity for the game. His father played ball with him whenever he could to help him improve his skills. They also spent a lot of time hunting and fishing together. His mother also helped in his development as a ballplayer. "I think memories that I'll have of my mother growing up," he said, "are going to be those of her out in the outfield, shagging flyballs, allowing me to get as many swings in during the course of the day as possible to give me every opportunity to get better and succeed. My mom was always there to support me no matter what I did."[69]

As an only child, Chipper received all of his parents' attention. Unlike many others, however, he was not spoiled. His father had grown up in a strict family and raised his son the same way. As his dad remembered, "I'd say once or twice a year, from the time Chipper was five or six until he was 13 or 14, I'd get out the belt. I gave the usual speech: 'This is going to hurt me a lot more than it's going to hurt you.' And Chipper would say, 'I won't do it again,' and I'd remember my father saying, 'If you let a child off once, it will be only harder the next time.' I think every now and then, pain is a powerful motivator. I firmly believe children will do what you demand of them, not what you ask of them."[70]

Chipper began playing organized ball in the DeLand/Pierson Minor League program when he was seven years old. He soon moved up to the Little League, where he became a dominating player. During one district playoff game, he slugged three home runs. It was around this time that his father realized Chipper had the potential to some day make it to the major leagues.

A High School Star

Chipper attended Taylor High School where he made the varsity team as a shortstop and pitcher while in the eighth grade (at the time, the school consisted of grades seven through twelve). Because of his athletic prowess, some of the teachers

started giving him preferential treatment. "By eighth and ninth grades," said his father, "we were seeing some signs that he was getting some breaks in school because he was such a good athlete. He was getting A's and B's, but we didn't see a lot of academic work at home. As much as we would tell his teachers that we didn't want them to cut him any breaks . . . we could tell he was getting a few cuts. And that's not the way life works."[71] After the ninth grade, they decided to transfer him to The Bolles School, a private boarding school in Jacksonville.

Larry Wayne "Chipper" Jones watches a ball leave Jack Murphy Stadium in San Diego during a 1995 game. Since becoming a regular for the Braves in 1994, Jones has been one of the top power hitters in the National League.

Although it was difficult being away from his friends and family at that age, Chipper eventually realized it was for the best. "It forced me to grow up," he wrote on his web site, "to overcome my fears and insecurities, to be challenged academically, and to play sports in a place where I wasn't already guaranteed a spot because of my past performance. It made me prove myself all over again, which was something I needed at the time."[72]

Chipper played baseball, football, and basketball at Bolles. He starred on coach Don Suriano's baseball squad, leading the school to the 2A State Championship in his senior year when he was honored as the Florida High School Player of the Year.

By the time he was eighteen, Chipper was regarded by many observers as the best amateur player in the nation. The Braves had the number one pick in the draft that year, and their first choice was high school pitching sensation Todd Van Poppel of

Texas. Prior to the draft, however, Van Poppel said that he would only sign with the Oakland A's. Rather than take the chance that they might not be able to sign him, Atlanta selected Jones instead. Said Braves' director of player personnel Paul Snyder, "We got the word early on Chipper that he wanted to sign; we never got the position cleared up with the other guy. That made our decision very easy. We already had a lot of pitching. That probably directed us in the way we should have gone anyway."[73]

The Braves offered Jones considerably less than he probably could have gotten. To Chipper, however, the value of the contract was secondary. "I don't care about the money," he told his father when the Braves made their offer. "I want to be playing professional baseball in two weeks."[74] He signed for $350,000 and began his pro career that summer with the Bradenton Braves of the Gulf Coast League.

Chipper Jones fields a grounder at third base. Jones was a shortstop in high school and in the Braves' minor-league farm system, but the team moved him to third base because of his strong arm.

Fulfilling His Promise

Chipper struggled in his rookie season at Bradenton, batting just .229. The next year, he began to fulfill his potential and show why he had been drafted so high. He hit .323 with fifteen home runs for Macon in 1991, then followed up with a solid season split between Durham and Greenville in 1992. The next year, he batted .325 for the Triple-A Richmond Braves and was named the organization's AAA Player of the Year. Jones was called up to the big-league club at the end of the season and got a pair of hits in three at bats in his first taste of major-league action.

During the offseason, Braves' leftfielder Ron Gant broke his leg in a motorcycle accident. When spring training came around, Jones was moved to left field and given Gant's place in the starting lineup. Unfortunately, he could not take advantage of his opportunity. On March 18, while playing an exhibition game against the New York Yankees, he tried to avoid a tag at first base and tore the anterior cruciate ligament in his left knee. Jones underwent surgery and was sidelined for the entire season. "It was my first summer ever without playing baseball," he remembered. "Just sitting there at home watching games on television, not being able to do anything, was very depressing."[75] He helped fight off his depression by working out in the weight room, where he added muscle to his six-foot three-inch, 200-pound body. When he reported to the team the next spring, he was ready to reclaim his spot in the lineup.

With David Justice taking over in left field, the Braves switched Jones to third base in order to take advantage of his strong arm. Despite the fact that he had only played shortstop in the minors, he had no problems adapting to the new position. "I've been an infielder all my life," he said. "As a shortstop, you need an arm, range and instincts—I have all of those. At third, you need an arm, but it's a position of reactions—I have those, too."[76]

The twenty-three-year-old rookie was inserted into the third spot in the batting order where he proceeded to justify manager Bobby Cox's faith in him. He batted .265 for the year while hitting 23 home runs and driving in 86 runs. He finished second in the Rookie of the Year voting, but had confidence that he could do even better. "By putting me in the three hole," he said, "Bobby wanted power and runs batted in. I did all right there, and .265 isn't that bad. But I still think I'm a .300 hitter in this league."[77]

Heading into the postseason, Jones did not seem at all nervous. As he explained, "I've been through a lot of pressure games in my life. Some guys live for crunch time. I'm one of them."[78] He proceeded to help the Braves dismantle the Colorado Rockies in the National League Division Series. In Game 1, he hit a pair of home runs, including what proved to be the game winner with two outs in the top half of the ninth inning. He also saved a run with a brilliant diving stop that turned a sure hit into a force play that resulted in an out. In Game 2, the Braves trailed by a run going into the ninth. Jones led off with a double, sparking a four-run rally that gave Atlanta the win. After Colorado won Game 3, 7-5 in ten innings, Jones helped Atlanta come back from a 3-0 deficit by doubling home two runs in the third inning of Game 4. The Braves went on to win, 10-4, to move into the National League Championship Series (NLCS) against the Reds. In his first playoff series ever, Jones batted a robust .389.

The Reds, too, felt Jones's wrath. In the Braves' four-game sweep of Cincinnati, he stroked seven hits in sixteen at bats for a .437 average. He also added another homer in Game 3.

Jones's production fell off somewhat in the World Series against the Cleveland Indians, but his .286 average was nothing to be ashamed of. All told, in fourteen postseason games, he collected twenty hits for a .364 batting average, with 5 doubles, 3 home runs, and 8 runs batted in. The Braves defeated the Indians in the Series, bringing Jones' first full year in the major leagues to a memorable conclusion.

A Rising Star

Prior to the start of the 1996 season, the Braves signed Jones to a four-year, $8.25 million contract. The contract provided him with security and also showed a commitment to him by the Braves. "This is the type of guy you build your young nucleus around,"[79] said general manager John Schuerholz.

Jones's production soared in 1999, when he blasted 45 homers and drove in 110 runs. He also batted .319, hit 41 doubles, stole 25 bases, and drew 126 walks—statistics that won him the league's MVP Award.

He started the year on the disabled list, but when he came off, he quickly showed that his rookie season was not a fluke. Jones reached the .300 mark for the first time, finishing the year at .309. He also clubbed 30 home runs, scored 114 runs, and drove home 110.

Jones improved on his NLCS heroics of the year before. He stroked eleven hits in twenty-five at bats against the Cardinals for a .440 batting average. He again hit .286 in the World Series, but the Braves could not repeat as champions. They lost to the New York Yankees in seven games.

A Personal Crisis

Jones had two more solid seasons in 1997 and 1998, batting .295 and .313, respectively. He became one of the leaders of the team, respected by his teammates for his unselfish attitude, humility, and solid work ethic. With his little-boy enthusiasm for the game and all-American good looks, he was also wildly popular with the fans. As Atlanta sports memorabilia dealer Bob Pressley put it, "He has the perfect image for baseball right now."[80] Unfortunately, that image was tarnished because of a mistake in judgment.

Jones had met Karin Fulford in 1991 and married her a year later. In spring training of 1997, he began having an affair with a waitress that resulted in a son being born out of wedlock in March 1998. When the news came out, Jones admitted his mistake and took responsibility for his actions. "I went public," he told Sports Illustrated's Tom Verducci, "partly because my wife pressured me to do it. But that was like a weight lifting off my shoulders. I had been living a hypocritical life. I wasn't as quick to look people in the eye, and I didn't want to do that anymore. That was the only good thing that came out of it. I cleared my conscience. I'm paying for my mistakes. I am greatly sorry for them. But I feel it's time to close the door."[81] With his marriage breaking up, Jones threw himself into a weight-training program and into preparing for the 1999 season.

Coming of Age

When Jones arrived in Kissimmee, Florida, for spring training the next year, he was approached by new Atlanta hitting coach, Don Baylor. Baylor told him he expected Jones to hit for more power. "You hit third for the best team in the National League," said Baylor, "and I expect you to drive the ball out of the park."[82]

Jones took Baylor's words to heart. After starting off slowly, he proceeded to put together one of the best seasons ever by a switch-hitter. He finished with career highs in home runs (45—a new National League record for switch-hitters), batting average (.319), stolen bases (25), and walks (126). Jones became the first player in major-league history to hit .300, score 100 runs, drive home 100 runs, hit 40 doubles and 40 home runs, draw 100 walks, and steal 25 bases in a season. Ironically, because of his slow start, he did not make the All-Star team. He did, however, win the National League Most Valuable Player Award for leading the Braves to the World Series.

Although Chipper Jones switched defensive positions after the 2001 season, moving to left field, his offensive production has remained consistent. Jones drove in 100 runs or more every year between 1996 and 2002.

Jones's value to the team was perhaps best exemplified by his performance in a late-season series against the New York Mets. He single-handedly killed off New York's pennant hopes by stroking four home runs and driving in seven runs in the Braves' three-game sweep. "He had an MVP season, no doubt about it," said manager Bobby Cox. "He deserves it and I'm happy for him."[83]

Since his MVP year, Jones has continued to add to his reputation as one of the best players in the game. Over the next three years, he batted .311, .330, and .327 while averaging just over 33 home runs and 104 runs batted in per season. He experienced some problems in the field in 2000 and 2001, however. He volunteered to move to left field and did so when the Braves acquired third baseman Vinny Castilla prior to the 2002 season.

A Bright Future

In eight full major league seasons, Jones has compiled a .309 batting average, with 253 home runs and 837 runs batted in. He has reached the 100 mark in RBIs for seven consecutive years and been selected for the All-Star Game five times. Remarkably consistent, Jones has also recorded a .309 batting average in ninety-four postseason games to go along with 10 home runs. If he continues along at his current pace, he will likely be a candidate for the Baseball Hall of Fame when his playing days are over.

In addition to spending time with his family (he remarried in 2000), Jones also donates much of his time to charity. In addition to working with the Georgia Chapter of the Cystic Fibrosis Foundation, he also established the Chipper Jones Family Foundation. Among other things, the Foundation works together with the Braves in refurbishing youth baseball fields in the Atlanta area. It has also set up an annual scholarship at Taylor High School in honor of Chipper's father.

Atlanta Braves Achievements

Year–by–Year Records

WS 1 = won the World Series   **NL 1** = won the league pennant
DIV 1 = won the division

Year	League	Record	Finish	Manager
2002	N.L. East	101–59	DIV 1	Cox
2001	N.L. East	88–74	DIV 1	Cox
2000	N.L. East	95–67	DIV 1	Cox
1999	N.L. East	103–59	NL 1	Cox
1998	N.L. East	106–56	DIV 1	Cox
1997	N.L. East	101–61	DIV 1	Cox
1996	N.L. East	96–66	NL 1	Cox
1995	N.L. East	90–54	WS 1	Cox
1994	N.L. East	68–46	2	Cox
1993	N.L. West	104–58	DIV 1	Cox
1992	N.L. West	98–64	NL 1	Cox
1991	N.L. West	94–68	NL 1	Cox
1990	N.L. West	65–97	6	Nixon/Cox
1989	N.L. West	63–97	6	Nixon
1988	N.L. West	54–106	6	Tanner/ Nixon
1987	N.L. West	69–92	5	Tanner
1986	N.L. West	72–89	6	Tanner
1985	N.L. West	66–96	5	Haas/Wine
1984	N.L. West	80–82	3	Torre
1983	N.L. West	88–74	2	Torre
1982	N.L. West	89–73	DIV 1	Torre
1981	N.L. West	50–56	—	Cox
1980	N.L. West	81–80	4	Cox
1979	N.L. West	66–94	6	Cox
1978	N.L. West	69–93	6	Cox
1977	N.L. West	61–101	6	Bristol/ Turner/ Benson

Year	League	Record	Finish	Manager
1976	N.L. West	70–92	6	Bristol
1975	N.L. West	67–94	5	King/Ryan
1974	N.L. West	88–74	3	Mathews/ King
1973	N.L. West	76–85	5	Mathews
1972	N.L. West	70–84	4	Harris/ Mathews
1971	N.L. West	82–80	3	Harris
1970	N.L. West	76–86	5	Harris
1969	N.L. West	93–69	DIV 1	Harris
1968	N.L.	81–81	5	Harris
1967	N.L.	77–85	7	Hitchcock/ Silvestri
1966	N.L.	85–77	5	Bragan/ Hitchcock
1965	N.L.	86–76	5	Bragan
1964	N.L.	88–74	5	Bragan
1963	N.L.	84–78	6	Bragan
1962	N.L.	86–76	5	Tebbetts
1961	N.L.	83–71	4	Dressen/ Tebbetts
1960	N.L.	88–66	2	Dressen
1959	N.L.	86–70	2	Haney
1958	N.L.	92–62	NL 1	Haney
1957	N.L.	95–59	WS 1	Haney
1956	N.L.	92–62	2	Grimm/ Haney
1955	N.L.	85–69	2	Grimm
1954	N.L.	89–65	3	Grimm
1953	N.L.	92–62	2	Grimm
1952	N.L.	64–89	7	Holmes/ Grimm
1951	N.L.	76–78	4	Southworth/ Holmes
1950	N.L.	83–71	4	Southworth
1949	N.L.	75–79	4	Southworth/ Cooney
1948	N.L.	91–62	NL 1	Southworth
1947	N.L.	86–68	3	Southworth
1946	N.L.	81–72	4	Southworth

Year	League	Record	Finish	Manager
1945	N.L.	67–85	6	Coleman/ Bissonette
1944	N.L.	65–89	6	Coleman
1943	N.L.	68–85	6	Coleman/ Stengel
1942	N.L.	59–89	7	Stengel
1941	N.L.	62–92	7	Stengel
1940	N.L.	65–87	7	Stengel
1939	N.L.	63–88	7	Stengel
1938	N.L.	77–75	5	Stengel
1937	N.L.	79–73	5	McKechnie
1936	N.L.	71–83	6	McKechnie
1935	N.L.	38–115	8	McKechnie
1934	N.L.	78–73	4	McKechnie
1933	N.L.	83–71	4	McKechnie
1932	N.L.	77–77	5	McKechnie
1931	N.L.	64–90	7	McKechnie
1930	N.L.	70–84	6	McKechnie
1929	N.L.	56–98	8	Fuchs
1928	N.L.	50–103	7	Slattery/ Hornsby
1927	N.L.	60–94	7	Bancroft
1926	N.L.	66–86	7	Bancroft
1925	N.L.	70–83	5	Bancroft
1924	N.L.	53–100	8	Bancroft
1923	N.L.	54–100	7	Mitchell
1922	N.L.	53–100	8	Mitchell
1921	N.L.	79–74	4	Mitchell
1920	N.L.	62–90	7	Stallings
1919	N.L.	57–82	6	Stallings
1918	N.L.	53–71	7	Stallings
1917	N.L.	72–81	6	Stallings
1916	N.L.	89–63	3	Stallings
1915	N.L.	83–69	2	Stallings
1914	N.L.	94–59	WS 1	Stallings
1913	N.L.	69–82	5	Stallings
1912	N.L.	52–101	8	Kling
1911	N.L.	44–107	8	Tenney
1910	N.L.	53–100	8	Lake

Year	League	Record	Finish	Manager
1909	N.L.	45–108	8	Bowerman/ Smith
1908	N.L.	63–91	6	Kelley
1907	N.L.	58–90	7	Tenney
1906	N.L.	49–102	8	Tenney
1905	N.L.	51–103	7	Tenney
1904	N.L.	55–98	7	Buckenberger
1903	N.L.	58–80	6	Buckenberger
1902	N.L.	73–64	3	Buckenberger
1901	N.L.	69–69	5	Selee
1900	N.L.	66–72	4	Selee
1899	N.L.	95–57	2	Selee
1898	N.L.	102–47	NL 1	Selee
1897	N.L.	93–39	NL 1	Selee
1896	N.L.	74–57	4	Selee
1895	N.L.	71–60	6	Selee
1894	N.L.	83–49	3	Selee
1893	N.L.	86–43	NL 1	Selee
1892	N.L.	102–48	WS 1	Selee
1891	N.L.	87–51	NL 1	Selee
1890	N.L.	76–57	5	Selee
1889	N.L.	83–45	2	Hart
1888	N.L.	70–64	4	Morrill
1887	N.L.	61–60	5	Kelly/Morrill
1886	N.L.	56–61	5	Morrill
1885	N.L.	46–66	5	Morrill
1884	N.L.	73–38	2	Morrill
1883	N.L.	63–35	NL 1	Burdock/ Morrill
1882	N.L.	45–39	4	Morrill
1881	N.L.	38–45	6	Wright
1880	N.L.	40–44	6	Wright
1879	N.L.	54–30	2	Wright
1878	N.L.	41–19	NL 1	Wright
1877	N.L.	42–18	NL 1	Wright
1876	N.L.	39–31	4	Wright

National League Year-by-Year Leaders

Wins

1945—Dick Barrett,	23
1948—Johnny Sain,	24
1949—Warren Spahn,	21
1950—Warren Spahn,	21
1953—Warren Spahn,	23*
1957—Warren Spahn,	21
1958—Warren Spahn,	22*
1959—Lew Burdette,	21*
1959—Warren Spahn,	21*
1960—Warren Spahn,	21*
1961—Warren Spahn,	21*
1974—Phil Niekro,	20*
1979—Phil Niekro,	21*
1991—Tom Glavine,	20*
1992—Tom Glavine,	20*
1993—Tom Glavine,	22*
1994—Greg Maddux,	16*
1995—Greg Maddux,	19
1996—John Smoltz,	24
1997—Denny Neagle,	20
1998—Tom Glavine,	20
2000—Tom Glavine,	21

*Tied for the league lead

Strikeouts

1902—Vic Willis,	225
1906—Big Jeff Pfeffer,	158
1949—Warren Spahn,	151
1950—Warren Spahn,	191
1951—Warren Spahn,	164*
1952—Warren Spahn,	183
1977—Phil Niekro,	262
1992—John Smoltz,	215
1996—John Smoltz,	276

*Tied for the league lead

Earned Run Average

1937—Jim Turner,	2.38
1947—Warren Spahn,	2.33
1951—Chet Nichols,	2.88
1953—Warren Spahn,	2.10
1956—Lew Burdette,	2.70
1961—Warren Spahn,	3.02
1967—Phil Niekro,	1.87
1974—Buzz Capra,	2.28
1993—Greg Maddux	2.36
1994—Greg Maddux	1.56
1995—Greg Maddux	1.63
1998—Greg Maddux	2.22

Home Runs

1907—Dave Brain,	10
1910—Fred Beck,	10*
1935—Wally Berger,	34
1945—Tommy Holmes,	28
1953—Eddie Mathews,	47
1957—Hank Aaron,	44
1959—Eddie Mathews,	46
1963—Hank Aaron,	44*
1966—Hank Aaron,	44
1967—Hank Aaron,	39
1984—Dale Murphy,	36*
1985—Dale Murphy,	37

*Tied for the league lead

Stolen Bases

1950—Sam Jethroe,	35
1951—Sam Jethroe,	35
1953—Bill Bruton,	26
1954—Bill Bruton,	34
1955—Bill Bruton,	25

Batting Average

1928—Rogers Hornsby, .387
1942—Ernie Lombardi, .330
1956—Hank Aaron,   .328
1959—Hank Aaron,   .355
1970—Rico Carty,   .366
1974—Ralph Garr,   .353
1991—Terry Pendleton, .319

Runs Batted In

1935—Wally Berger,   130
1957—Hank Aaron,   132
1960—Hank Aaron,   126
1963—Hank Aaron,   130
1966—Hank Aaron,   127
1982—Dale Murphy,   109*
1983—Dale Murphy,   121*

*Tied for the league lead

Braves Award Winners

Most Valuable Player Award

1947—Bob Elliott
1957—Hank Aaron
1982—Dale Murphy
1983—Dale Murphy
1991—Terry Pendleton
1999—Chipper Jones

Rookie of the Year Award

1948—Alvin Dark
1950—Sam Jethroe
1971—Earl Williams
1978—Bob Horner

1990—David Justice
2000—Rafael Furcal

Manager of the Year Award

1991—Bobby Cox

Cy Young Award

1957—Warren Spahn
1991—Tom Glavine
1993—Greg Maddux
1994—Greg Maddux
1995—Greg Maddux
1996—John Smoltz
1998—Tom Glavine

Notes

Chapter 1: Three Cities, Three Championships

1. Quoted in Bob Klapisch and Pete Van Wieren, *The Braves*. Atlanta, GA: Turner Publishing, 1996, p. 27.
2. Quoted in Gary Caruso, *The Braves Encyclopedia*. Philadelphia, PA: Temple University Press, 1995, p. 39.
3. Quoted in Caruso, *The Braves Encyclopedia*, p. 394.
4. Quoted in Klapisch and Van Wieren, *The Braves*, p. 163.
5. Quoted in Klapisch and Van Wieren, *The Braves*, p. 165.

Chapter 2: Hank Aaron

6. Quoted in David Pietrusza, Matthew Silverman, and Michael Gershman, eds., *Baseball: The Biographical Encyclopedia*. New York: Total/Sports Illustrated, 2000, p. 1.
7. Hank Aaron with Lonnie Wheeler, *I Had A Hammer*. New York: HarperCollins, 1991, p. 21.
8. Quoted in Caruso, *The Braves Encyclopedia*, p. 136.
9. Quoted in Pietrusza, Silverman, and Gershman, eds., *Baseball: The Biographical Encyclopedia*, p. 2.
10. Quoted in Klapisch and Van Wieren, *The Braves*, p. 114.
11. Quoted in Klapisch and Van Wieren, *The Braves*, p. 115.
12. Quoted in Caruso, *The Braves Encyclopedia*, p. 137.
13. Aaron with Wheeler, *I Had A Hammer*, p. 147.
14. Aaron with Wheeler, *I Had A Hammer*, p. 181.
15. Quoted in John Holway, ed., *The Sluggers*. Alexandria, VA: Redefinition, 1989, p. 74.
16. Quoted in Klapisch and Van Wieren, *The Braves*, p. 157.
17. Quoted in Wayne Minshew, "The Hammer Hits the Big One," *The Sporting News*, April 27, 1974.
18. Quoted in Klapisch and Van Wieren, *The Braves*, p. 161.
19. Aaron with Wheeler, *I Had A Hammer*, pp. 332–33.

Chapter 3: Phil Niekro

20. Quoted in Steve Wulf, "Knucksie Hasn't Lost His Grip," *Sports Illustrated*, June 4, 1984, p. 96.
21. Quoted in Ron Fimrite, "The Valley Boys," *Sports Illustrated*, May 23, 1988, p. 84.
22. Quoted in Fimrite, "The Valley Boys," p. 84.
23. Quoted in Wulf, "Knucksie Hasn't Lost His Grip," p. 98.
24. Quoted in Wulf, "Knucksie Hasn't Lost His Grip," p. 98.
25. Phil Niekro and Tom Bird, *Knuckle Balls*. New York: Freundlich Books, 1986, p. 19.
26. Quoted in Anthony Dasher, "Niekro to Speak At Diamond Club Jamboree," *Athens Banner-Herald*, January 31, 1998.
27. Quoted in Associated Press, "Niekro Saddened by Demise of Silver Bullets," *Athens Banner-Herald*, April, 21, 1998.
28. Quoted in Dasher, "Niekro to Speak At Diamond Club Jamboree."

Chapter 4: Dale Murphy

29. Quoted in Rick Reilly, "So Good, He's Scary," *Sports Illustrated*, June 3, 1985, p. 82.
30. Quoted in Joe Strauss, "Murphy: 'This Was Saying Goodbye,'" *The Atlanta Journal-Constitution*, June 14, 1994, p. C6.
31. Quoted in Steve Wulf, "Murphy's Law Is Nice Guys Finish First," *Sports Illustrated*, July 4, 1983.
32. Quoted in Malcolm Moran, "Murphy Is Confident, at Last," *The New York Times*, May 17, 1983.
33. Quoted in Tim Tucker, "Complete Player: Dale Murphy," *The Sporting News*, September 20, 1982, p. 3.
34. Quoted in Wulf, "Murphy's Law Is Nice Guys Finish First."
35. Quoted in Peter Gammons, "A Man Who Can't Say No," *Sports Illustrated*, December 21, 1987.
36. Quoted in Vic Fulp, "Throwing Flaws Block Path Back to Majors for Murphy," *The Sporting News*, May 7, 1977, p. 29.
37. Quoted in Tucker, "Complete Player: Dale Murphy," p.3.
38. Quoted in Wulf, "Murphy's Law Is Nice Guys Finish First."
39. Quoted in Wulf, "Murphy's Law Is Nice Guys Finish First."
40. Quoted in Robbie Andreu, "Dale Murphy Turned into Mere

Mortal Last Season," *Fort Lauderdale News & Sun-Sentinel*, March 15, 1987.

41. Quoted in Scott Miller, "Dale Murphy's Class Act Moves to Philadelphia," *Baseball Hobby News*, October 1990, p. 12.

42. Quoted in Miller, "Dale Murphy's Class Act Moves to Philadelphia," p. 12.

43. Quoted in Miller, "Dale Murphy's Class Act Moves to Philadelphia," p. 12.

44. Quoted in Tim Tucker, "Dale Murphy Ends Mission, Returns to Atlanta for All-Star Game," *The Atlanta Journal-Constitution*, July 9, 2000.

45. Quoted in Elizabeth Carlston, "Dale Murphy: Baseball MVP, Mission President, Governor?" *NewsNet*, January 21, 2003.

46. Quoted in Wulf, "Murphy's Law Is Nice Guys Finish First."

Chapter 5: Tom Glavine

47. Tom Glavine with Nick Cafardo, *None but the Braves*. New York: HarperCollins 1996, p. 19–20.

48. Quoted in Leigh Montville, "A Gripping Tale," *Sports Illustrated*, July 13, 1992, p. 44.

49. Quoted in Glavine with Cafardo, None but the Braves. p. 25.

50. Quoted in Montville, "A Gripping Tale," p. 43.

51. Glavine with Cafardo, *None but the Braves*. p. 42.

52. Glavine with Cafardo, *None but the Braves*. pp. 58–59.

53. Quoted in Steve Rushin, "Five Aces," *Sports Illustrated*, April 5, 1993, p. 38–39.

54. Quoted in Steve Marantz, "The Two Sides of Tom Glavine," *The Sporting News*, May 1, 1995.

55. Quoted in Marantz, "The Two Sides of Tom Glavine."

56. Quoted in Glavine with Cafardo, *None but the Braves*. p. xi.

57. Quoted in Montville, "A Gripping Tale," p. 44.

58. Quoted in Tom Verducci, "Both Sides Now," *Sports Illustrated*, June 17, 2002, p. 70.

59. Quoted in "Glavine Heads North to Join Mets," *ESPN*, December 5, 2002, www.espn.go.com.

Chapter 6: Greg Maddux

60. Quoted in James C. Roberts, "King of the Mound," *The World & I*, October 1996.

61. Quoted in Roberts, "King of the Mound."
62. Quoted in Tom Verducci, "Drive for Show, Pitch for Dough," *Sports Illustrated*, May 1, 1995, p. 115.
63. Quoted in Michael P. Geffner, "'I Just Pitch,'" *The Sporting News*, October 9, 1995.
64. Quoted in Verducci, "Drive for Show, Pitch for Dough," p. 116.
65. Quoted in Judith Graham, ed., *Current Biography Yearbook: 1996*. New York: H.W. Wilson, 1996, p. 337.
66. Quoted in Roberts, "King of the Mound."
67. Quoted in Roberts, "King of the Mound."

Chapter 7: Chipper Jones

68. Quoted in Michael Bamberger, "Riding High," *Sports Illustrated*, September 16, 1996, p. 62.
69. Quoted in Mark Bowman, "Memories of Mom's Contributions," *Atlanta Braves*, www.braves.mlb.com.
70. Quoted in Bamberger, "Riding High," p. 66.
71. Quoted in Steve Hummer, "Bravo for Chipper," *The Sporting News 1996 Baseball Yearbook*, p. 40.
72. The Official Website of Chipper Jones (www.chipperjones.com).
73. Quoted in Hummer, "Bravo for Chipper," p. 39.
74. Quoted in Bamberger, "Riding High," p. 66.
75. Quoted in Dave Kindred, "He's Got the Good Face—And More," *The Sporting News*, October 16, 1995, p. 6.
76. Quoted in Tim Kurkjian, "Cashing in the Chip," *Sports Illustrated*, June 5, 1995, p. 78.
77. Quoted in Kindred, "He's Got the Good Face—And More," p. 6.
78. Quoted in Tim Kurkjian, "Pressure-Treated," *Sports Illustrated*, October 16, 1995, p. 26.
79. Quoted in Pete Williams, "A Blue-Chip Prospect," *Baseball Weekly*, July 24–30, 1996.
80. Quoted in Williams, "A Blue-Chip Prospect."
81. Quoted in Tom Verducci, "Switched On!" *Sports Illustrated*, October 4, 1999, p. 49.
82. Quoted in Verducci, "Switched On!" p. 44.
83. Quoted in Bill Zack, "Chipper Jones Has NL MVP Locked Up," *Savannah Morning News*, November 9, 1999.

For Further Reading

Gary Caruso, *Turner Field: Rarest of Diamonds*. Atlanta, GA: Longstreet Press, 1997. A history of Turner Field, home of the Atlanta Braves since 1997.

Donald Dewey and Nicholas Acocella, *The Biographical History of Baseball*. New York: Carroll and Graf, 1995. A biographical resource summarizing the contributions of over fifteen hundred players, managers, and executives to the game of baseball.

Josh Leventhal, *The World Series: An Illustrated Encyclopedia of the Fall Classic*. New York: Black Dog & Leventhal, 2002. A comprehensive tribute to baseball's Fall Classic, updated through the 2002 season.

Lawrence T. Lorimer, *Baseball Desk Reference*. New York: DK Publishing, 2002. This comprehensive volume of over six hundred pages was written in collaboration with the National Baseball Hall of Fame Museum.

Geoffrey C. Ward and Ken Burns, *Baseball: An Illustrated History*. New York: Alfred A. Knopf, 1994. This lavishly illustrated book is the companion volume to the PBS television series of the same name.

Works Consulted

Books

Hank Aaron with Lonnie Wheeler, *I Had A Hammer.* New York: HarperCollins, 1991. The autobiography of baseball's all-time home run champion.

Gary Caruso, *The Braves Encyclopedia.* Philadelphia, PA: Temple University Press, 1995. A comprehensive encyclopedia of the Braves from the franchise's inception in 1871 up through the 1994 season.

Tom Glavine with Nick Cafardo, *None but the Braves.* New York: HarperCollins, 1996. The autobiography of the Braves stylish lefty who was the winningest pitcher in the nineties.

Judith Graham, ed., *Current Biography Yearbook: 1996.* New York: H.W. Wilson, 1996. Library volume that contains all of the biographies published in the *Current Biography* magazine in 1996.

John Holway, ed., *The Sluggers.* Alexandria, VA: Redefinition, 1989. This volume in Redefinition's World of Baseball series examines the long-ball hitters who have excited fans through the years.

Bob Klapisch and Pete Van Wieren, *The Braves.* Atlanta, GA: Turner Publishing, 1996. An illustrated history of the Braves, tracing the team's travels from Boston to Milwaukee to Atlanta.

Phil Niekro and Tom Bird, *Knuckle Balls.* New York: Freundlich Books, 1986. Hall of Fame pitcher Phil Niekro's own account of his years with the New York Yankees.

David Pietrusza, Matthew Silverman, and Michael Gershman, eds., *Baseball: The Biographical Encyclopedia.* New York: Total/Sports Illustrated, 2000. This volume contains essays on more than two thousand of the most talented players, managers, umpires, executives, and journalists associated with the game of baseball.

Periodicals

Robbie Andreu, "Dale Murphy Turned into Mere Mortal Last Season," *Fort Lauderdale News & Sun-Sentinel*, March 15, 1987.

Associated Press, "Niekro Saddened by Demise of Silver Bullets," *Athens Banner-Herald*, April, 21, 1998.

Michael Bamberger, "Riding High," *Sports Illustrated*, September 16, 1996, pp. 60–66.

Elizabeth Carlston, "Dale Murphy: Baseball MVP, Mission President, Governor?" *NewsNet*, January 21, 2003.

Anthony Dasher, "Niekro to Speak at Diamond Club Jamboree," *Athens Banner-Herald*, January 31, 1998.

Ron Fimrite, "The Valley Boys," *Sports Illustrated*, May 23, 1988, pp. 78–92.

Vic Fulp, "Throwing Flaws Block Path Back to Majors for Murphy," *Sporting News*, May 7, 1977, p. 29.

Peter Gammons, "A Man Who Can't Say No," *Sports Illustrated*, December 21, 1987, p. 16–17.

Michael P. Geffner, "'I Just Pitch,'" *Sporting News*, October 9, 1995.

Joe Hawk, "Ace of Diamonds," *Las Vegas Review-Journal*, December 31, 1999.

Steve Hummer, "Bravo for Chipper," *Sporting News 1996 Baseball Yearbook*, pp. 38–40.

Dave Kindred, "He's Got the Good Face—And More," *Sporting News*, October 16, 1995, p. 6.

Tim Kurkjian, "Cashing in the Chip," *Sports Illustrated*, June 5, 1995, pp. 78–79.

Tim Kurkjian, "Pressure-Treated," *Sports Illustrated*, October 16, 1995, pp. 26–27.

Steve Marantz, "The Two Sides of Tom Glavine," *Sporting News*, May 1, 1995.

Scott Miller, "Dale Murphy's Class Act Moves to Philadelphia," *Baseball Hobby News*, October 1990, p. 12.

Wayne Minshew, "The Hammer Hits the Big One," *Sporting News*, April 27, 1974.

Leigh Montville, "A Gripping Tale," *Sports Illustrated*, July 13, 1992, pp. 42–45.

Malcolm Moran, "Murphy Is Confident, at Last," *New York Times*, May 17, 1983.

Rick Reilly, "So Good, He's Scary," *Sports Illustrated*, June 3, 1985, pp. 75–88.

James C. Roberts, "King of the Mound," *World & I*, October 1996.

Steve Rushin, "Five Aces," *Sports Illustrated*, April 5, 1993, pp. 34–41.

Joe Strauss, "Murphy: 'This Was Saying Goodbye,'" *Atlanta Journal-Constitution*, June 14, 1994, p. C6.

Tim Tucker, "Complete Player: Dale Murphy," *Sporting News*, September 20, 1982, p. 3.

Tim Tucker, "Dale Murphy Ends Mission, Returns to Atlanta for All-Star Game," *Atlanta Journal-Constitution*, July 9, 2000.

Tom Verducci, "Both Sides Now," *Sports Illustrated*, June 17, 2002, pp. 68–72.

———, "Drive for Show, Pitch for Dough," *Sports Illustrated*, May 1, 1995, pp. 110– 119.

———, "Once in a Lifetime," *Sports Illustrated*, August 14, 1995, pp. 22–30.

———, "Switched on!" *Sports Illustrated*, October 4, 1999, pp. 44–49.

Pete Williams, "A Blue-Chip Prospect," *Baseball Weekly*, July 24–30, 1996.

Steve Wulf, "Knucksie Hasn't Lost His Grip," *Sports Illustrated*, June 4, 1984, pp. 90–104.

Steve Wulf, "Murphy's Law Is Nice Guys Finish First," *Sports Illustrated*, July 4, 1983, pp. 24–31.

Bill Zack, "Chipper Jones Has NL MVP Locked Up," *Savannah Morning News*, November 9, 1999.

Internet Sources

Mark Bowman, "Memories of Mom's Contributions," *Atlanta Braves*, www.braves.mlb.com.

"Glavine Heads North to Join Mets," *ESPN*, December 5, 2002, www.espn.go.com.

Websites

The Official Website of Chipper Jones (www.chipperjones.com). The official Website of the Braves' All-Star third baseman-outfielder.

Index

Picture Credits

About the Author

John F. Grabowski is a native of Brooklyn, New York. He holds a bachelor's degree in psychology from City College of New York and a master's degree in educational psychology from Teacher's College, Columbia University. He has been a teacher for thirty-three years, as well as a freelance writer, specializing in the fields of sports, education, and comedy. His body of published work includes thirty-eight books; a nationally syndicated sports column; consultation on several math textbooks; articles for newspapers, magazines, and the programs of professional sports teams; and comedy material sold to Jay Leno, Joan Rivers, Yakov Smirnoff, and numerous other comics. He and his wife, Patricia, live in Staten Island with their daughter, Elizabeth.